D0498147

WHAT'S LEFT OF THE LABOUR PARTY?

What's Left
of the
Labour Party?

WOODROW WYATT

SIDGWICK & JACKSON
LONDON

First published in Great Britain in 1977
by Sidgwick and Jackson Limited

Copyright © 1977 Woodrow Wyatt

ISBN 0 283 98427 9

Printed in Great Britain by
The Garden House Press Limited, London
for Sidgwick and Jackson Limited
1 Tavistock Chambers, Bloomsbury Way
London WC1 2SG

CONTENTS

THE LAWS of libel have prevented me from naming individuals as Communists or crypto-Communists, who have not declared themselves as such. Many Left Wing extremists are not Communists but consider themselves to be Marxists. Some Left Wing extremists do not even think of themselves as Marxists and some may call themselves International Socialists or Trotskyists or some other name of a group or outlook contained within the ultra-Left. Some who take an extremist attitude even believe that their aims could be achieved without destroying democracy. It is difficult precisely to pinpoint the exact brand of belief of all those gathered in the ultra-Left or who give aid to it, partially or wholly, wittingly or unwittingly. Hence I have not used any one description of people on the very Left Wing of the Labour Party, or just outside it and trying to infiltrate into it. They do not always agree among themselves though they are united in wishing to eliminate Social Democrats from power and influence in the Labour Party and in the trade unions.

CHAPTER ONE

The Millennium is Sighted

I JOINED the Labour Party nearly thirty-five years ago. Between 1945 and 1970 I was a Labour Member of Parliament for over twenty-one years. During all that time I subscribed, with some qualifications, to the policies of the Labour Party and its Governments. Why am I now disenchanted? Have I changed? Has the Labour Party changed? Have circumstances changed?

Many thousands who were once fervently pro-Labour now have doubts. With those doubts comes a faint feeling of guilt. The Labour Party is not an ordinary political party. It has not gathered support solely on acceptance of a series of pragmatic proposals to deal with the problems of the immediate future. It is more like a Church in which faith and hope and an irrational belief in the willingness of human beings to be good are the ingredients of the Gospel.

Its articulate enemies are not merely mistaken: they are sinful. Members of the Labour Party are brethren in a continuing religious revival. They may say and do bitter things to each other when they dispute about doctrine but there is no question of there not being a doctrine however impossible it is to pin it down or to define it. All who join the Labour Party, and to a lesser but real extent who believe in it without joining it, are comrades in the struggle for abstract as well as material good.

Withdrawal from the Labour Party implies a wider disloyalty from that involved in changing between the old Conservative and Liberal Parties. They had no religious quality about them and no commitment to fundamental changes in the way society was run. Disagreement over, for instance, the best way to deal with the Corn Laws or Home

7

Rule for Ireland could lead to a change of allegiance without a queasy feeling that an old moral faith was being betrayed.

It is hard to leave the Labour Party after a long involvement. Departure hints at a loss of idealism and suggests an admission of being foolishly mistaken in much that one has previously said and done. The longtime Labour supporter cannot turn away without more than a twinge of regret for those in the ranks he leaves behind who will be wounded by his going. He feels vulnerable to the charge of inconsistency.

But a long support of the Labour Party as it was and a belief that it achieved much that was good can be quite consistent with a realization that most of its goodness has now evaporated. There can be no shame in ceasing to back an engine for improvement when it becomes an engine for destruction. It was right to support the Labour Party in the past. It is wrong to do so now and in the immediate future. My purpose is to explain why, in the hope that no faithful Labour supporter will feel that his character, his sense of decency or his mind has deteriorated because for the first time he is contemplating not voting Labour.

The idealistic erstwhile Labour voter who changes allegiance need not feel that he has turned away from the dreams he may have had for a just society. They remain as relevant, or irrelevant, as they ever were. But in my course through the Labour Party I have seen us come to the point where measures intended to create more justice have led to less justice. Idealism must, like technology, keep up to date if it is to have value. Idealism must understand that what looks good in concept can have unexpected and undesirable effects.

Now that the making of idealistic statements on behalf of the Labour Party has fallen, into the hands of those who believe that democracy and the liberty of the individual are secondary to a theoretical reorganization which, because it cannot be made to work satisfactorily, is certain to produce less, not more, general wealth than before, then that perverted idealism is worse than ineffective for achieving the aims it declares. It has become a force which could be the agent of widespread misery. The harder we pursue the just society armed with old-fashioned ideas now proved fallacious the further away we get from it.

There have been many attempts to draw up plans for a just society. They have foundered because a perfect balance of fairness between one individual and another cannot be defined with general agreement and cannot be maintained in practice. It is easier to recognize an unjust society than to abolish injustice.

Yet before the 1939 war Britain though tolerant and democratic was clearly a society in which injustice was so prevalent that it needed major correction. The exceptional, whatever their origins, could become Prime Ministers, millionaires, rich barristers, eminent architects, famous writers, artists, musicians and actors. But they had to be exceptional if they were to succeed without inherited riches or the nurturing of an educated middle-class background.

There was never an insurmountable bar to mobility between the classes, official or social, but the transition was remarkably hard. For the talented this of itself was often a valuable spur. The determination required to rise had to be developed at an early age and stayed with them all their life.

For several centuries few really able and ambitious people have been denied success by a hostile environment in Britain. Many were the better for the struggle. That is why Britain recurringly produced outstanding leaders, industrialists, inventors and colonial administrators.

But what about the rest? The obstacles to the person of average or limited qualities were usually too great for him to surmount. He was left, in relation to the talented, in a disproportionately depressed state. There was opportunity, but not equal opportunity. The leaders, whether through inheritance or their own endeavours or a combination of both, lived agreeably. The division between them and the great mass of the people, without whose support they could do little, grew.

Differing standards of comfort and availability of education between the classes were much less pronounced in medieval times than they gradually became in the eighteenth, nineteenth and early twentieth centuries. The family in the small Norman or early English manor house did not live in vastly grander style than their tenants and workers. The later gap between the large country and town houses and the cottages and slums was far greater.

For too long too little thought was given to how the poorer majority, mainly poor not from defects of character, lived. It was not unkindness but belief that Governments could do nothing about it which prompted the indifference. Nature, it was presumed, had to take its course.

Nature did take its course and very ugly it often was. The jungle has no attractive scheme of ethics, as those who get lost in it discover. The hope of civilizing the jungle of human relations has inspired the authors of the economic Utopias with which the world has been deluged. But it takes a long time for a stable society to realize how unjust it is and still longer to persuade it that something can and should be done significantly to reduce the injustice.

But when the disparity between sections of a community becomes provocatively great and affects many millions the conditions for an upheaval are present. Dictatorships can avert or delay such upheavals by preventing information circulating, or by consistent distortion of the facts and by repression.

The mass of Russians do not know that their life could be much easier if their society were organized differently. They do not know that in Western Europe the unemployed live incomparably better than the average Russian citizen at work. They do not know that the favoured few among them live like rich Western capitalists at a level far more remote from theirs than the Western capitalist's is from a Western factory worker. Those who have a glimmering of the truth and proclaim it are rapidly removed to a prison camp or a lunatic asylum. The lid can be kept down by repression for decades, perhaps centuries, if the oppressors are sufficiently confident, well organized and determined.

Before the last war, in Britain the most trivial excesses of the rich were published in the gossip columns. It was increasingly difficult to conceal injustice and unfairness. There was no hindrance to criticism of the manner in which we conducted our affairs.

During the war awareness raced on. The Army Bureau of

Current Affairs was a powerful force in revealing to hundreds of thousands of servicemen, and hence to their families, the inequitable nature of our society. War itself accelerates change in democracies.

Many people of my age and equivalent educational background, who meant to do something in and about the world and optimistically assumed they had the ability to do it, were infected by what they had discovered by human contact, as well as through writings, about the state of Britain. It was difficult for those with any sensitivity about the condition of their fellow countrymen to shut out a strong feeling that injustice was so great that it must be remedied.

It seemed to many of us that it was those at the top who had foolishly led us into war and had criminally neglected the elimination of gross inequalities in living backgrounds and in opportunities. Such men, we thought, could not be trusted with, or be expected to welcome, the drastic changes needed to avoid hideous disturbances. The dominant leaders were fixed in our minds as the Conservatives. We ignored the evident failures of the two minority Labour Governments or ascribed them to the machinations of Conservative financiers and industrialists. There was no hope of fairness or any version of a just society from those who had been pre-eminent in the exercise of power in Britain.

With so much unfairness in the system it was enough to demand that unfairness should be got rid of. Once unfairness had gone fairness and justice and equality of opportunity would reign. Minimum wages, adequate housing, improved and extended education, the abolition of nepotism, and countless other admirable objectives had only to be achieved to make everyone happy.

'We wish,' ran the declaration of the forty-seven anarchists arrested after the failure of their uprising at Lyon in 1870, 'in a word, equality – equality in fact as a corollary, or, rather as a primordial condition of liberty. From each according to his faculties, to each according to his needs.'

That seemed obvious common sense not diminished by the substitution of 'abilities' for 'faculties' by Karl Marx in

11

1875. Who, with a Christian upbringing, could resist such a proposition applied to politics? Youth brushes aside difficulties and believes in the nobility of human nature. To set about the task was to be half way to accomplishing it.

That was the reasoning which at that time brought me and many others similar to me to support the Labour Party. The immediate future cried out for progress, and the Conservative Party, however kindly many of its members might be, did not sound as though it was interested in progress, or at any rate in more than a teaspoonful at a time. The Liberals then, as today, seemed diffuse in purpose and incapable of coherent action. They had the air of would-be Socialists too snobbish to join the Labour Party. And, until well after 1945, most of the middle classes thought it not only revolutionary but morally disreputable to support the Labour Party. So for those with my kind of views Labour it had to be.

But not with revolutionary intent. What little I had read of Marx I found boring and old-fashioned. Stafford Cripps, thought of before the war as a firebrand of Socialism, once told me that he had never read *Das Kapital* and never would. In a letter to *The Times* in December 1976 Sir William Hayter, former British Ambassador to the Soviet Union, recalled a breakfast conversation with Attlee when he was staying with him at the Embassy in Moscow. 'Have you read Karl Marx?' Attlee asked. Sir William replied nervously that he had read the potted version supplied by the Foreign Office. 'Haven't read a word of it myself,' Attlee said.

Contrary to recently propagated theories designed to make respectable Trotskyists and other extremists in the Labour Party, Marxism was never significant in the thinking of those who built the Labour Party and of those who ran the Labour Government of 1945–51. Reform, the removal of the worst injustices, the creation of equal opportunities, the improvement of living standards for all in, and with the consent of, a democratic society were the aims – not revolution and dictatorship.

War brings out the most in everyone, or nearly everyone. Good and evil attributes are accentuated. In Britain where

12

there is so much innate goodness and decency that is an advantage. In the last war the hard-faced men who did so well out of the 1914-18 war seemed not to be so much about.

There was a high degree of fairness from the start. Conscription was universal though it was possible to enlist before being called up. The Government decided who should be in reserved occupations outside the armed forces so there was no disgrace in not wearing a uniform.

Rationing of food, clothing and other essentials, accompanied by price controls and enforced Government standards of quality, tended towards an egalitarian atmosphere. No one was seen to live in gross luxury while others suffered the hardships of war. The diet for millions actually improved and children began to grow up healthier than they had ever been previously. The reduced consumption of animal fats actually reduced the tendency to coronary diseases.

There were genuine feelings of unity. There was a general desire to put the country first. Class enmity or envy lessened. The rich were not automatically assumed to be having a cushy time, and tenants promoted from slums to council houses were no longer believed to keep coal in their baths. The bombing of London and other major cities meant dangers more evenly shared. The soldier in a theatre of war could frequently be safer than civilians bombed nightly.

A public school education might put a soldier on the road to a commission but he didn't get one unless he passed uniformly applied tests. The proportion of officers who were not from the middle class was much higher than in the First World War. Merit, rather than privilege, was the basis for advancement.

Some civilian jobs like mining were recognized as being as important as fighting. Many who would have preferred to be in the forces were directed to work in the mines. Labour was directed not for the profit of the employee or employer but for usefulness to the State.

The old argument that nothing worked effectively without a profit motive lost its force. Most people worked as hard as they could to help the country and thereby each other. Understanding between groups of different backgrounds diminished hostility, though it could not eradicate it.

Most extraordinary of all there was much less discontent. Most people enjoyed working for a common purpose. Direction into what you did might be compulsory but jobs were done with a voluntary enthusiasm. Never was Britain more one nation. People found fulfilment in putting the general good at least level with their own, if not above it.

This was certainly so in the Army. I had assumed that Regular Army officers would be class-conscious and indifferent to the feelings and needs of the soldiers. There was some evidence of this among officers from the Territorial Army, many of whom had volunteered for their commissions before the war for business purposes. A Territorial Army officers' mess had a touch of the chamber of commerce or golf club about it. But Regular Army officers had quite a different outlook.

In the main they put the soldiers before themselves. A second lieutenant who had a bath and a drink before seeing that his soldiers were comfortable after a route march was promptly rebuked and shamed. It was the second lieutenant's job not merely to make friends of the soldiers in his platoon but to listen to their worries and sort out their personal problems, much as the conscientious M.P. does with his constituents today. That was one way in which so many junior officers came to understand with their hearts as well as their minds the difficulties of the poor and the held down. Discipline in the Army was necessarily strict but it was generally humane. Officers did not ask soldiers to do things they were not prepared to do themselves however physically laborious or dangerous.

The tradition of the Regular Army involved earning the trust of the soldiers by example and fair dealing. In some respects the atmosphere was that of a well conducted public school based on the Christian ethic of thinking of others first. There was very little injustice. Everyone had their rights and some means of maintaining them. Life in the Army when one was not actually being fired upon or shelled was tolerable.

But the Regular Army believed not merely in selflessness

14

and respecting the individuality of others: it believed in efficiency. For before the war the small volunteer Army had had to make the most of its small resources to be comparable with the giant conscript armies on the Continent. Good man-management was the means which enabled efficiency to be obtained. But that could only be secured by careful planning.

The officers of the Regular Army were not fools, though on the whole they were not brilliant. Their planning was careful and sound. They were taught to define problems, state their objectives, consider the alternatives, detail and coordinate their plan of action. By adhering to rules evolved over a long period they were surprisingly good administrators. Moving and accommodating suddenly large numbers of men had become easy to them. Difficulties of bringing supplies over obstacles and long distances were nearly always overcome.

The Army medical services utilized their equipment, doctors, nurses and orderlies more effectively than any section of the National Health Service does now and with far less waste. The food was always there and well cooked in adverse conditions. The Army postal service hardly ever made a mistake and was swift in delivery. Relatives of the wounded, missing or killed were rapidly and sympathetically informed.

Whenever we were alongside American troops it was obvious that their greater wealth made their food and clothing better than ours. But they never matched the British Army in getting so much out of so little. The American Army seemed clumsy and cumbrous. It lacked the lean efficiency and quick responsiveness of the British Army.

The analogy with America seemed clear. The Americans could afford to waste because they had everything they needed in abundance. Vast U.S.A., nearly forty times the size of Britain with a population only about four times as great was more than self-sufficient. Oil, coal, and most minerals, almost everything required for manufacture, was within her own frontiers. Spreading farmlands still not even used to capacity gave her all her own food. Shortage of labour in the

East as factory workers were tempted to the West by free or cheap land had early forced upon America labour-saving machinery even today resisted in Britain for fear of unemployment.

In so huge a country enough for everyone could be produced without much planning. A fairer distribution of wealth and opportunity was not urgently necessary in America. With no constraints on the creation of more wealth any individual who chose could help himself at his own initiative. True, there had been the depression of the 1930s but America's riches and wartime production had enabled her to buy herself out of depression into prosperity on a scale not open to Britain.

Britain's position was very different. The tiny islands had neither the soil nor the climate to yield as much as a half of the food she needed. She had no oil. A much higher proportion of raw materials for industry had to be imported than in America.

When the Industrial Revolution started in 1750 the population of England and Wales was $6^{1}/_{3}$ million. By 1945 it was $42^{2}/_{3}$ million. At the beginning of their industrial development the British could provide most of their raw materials and food. Their ingenuity in engineering and manufacture earned them a standard of living from abroad which could not possibly have been generated within the shores of Britain alone. The British Empire had also contributed by providing cheap food and raw materials and a tied British export market.

Even during the war it was becoming obvious that this situation was of the past not of the future. Britain's very success as a nation exporting goods and services had stimulated her population to grow far larger than Britain could adequately maintain from her own resources. It was also inevitable that the British Empire would cease to be a captive market and to provide a buyer's market for raw materials sold to Britain.

Churchill had grandly declared on 10 November 1942, 'I have not become the King's First Minister in order to preside over the liquidation of the British Empire.' But those who thought about it realized that this was exactly what he was doing whatever his intentions. As he fought against the Government of India Act (1935) he must have known that the end was coming and could not be avoided though it might be delayed.

There was no convincing indication in 1945 that British management and employees had become inferior in skills or energy to their counterparts in America. That was to come later. But it was impossible for Britain to keep indefinitely the early lead she had won with her Industrial Revolution. Britain's share of the world export market would decline and was bound to continue to decline after the war.

Another difficulty in Britain had become the ever-escalating size of the finances needed to promote technical advances. Already by the Second World War British inventions were increasingly developed abroad because of the lack of capital and material resources in Britain. The atom was first split at Cambridge. But the weight of research and material to turn that British discovery into an atomic bomb could only be found in America. It was not just Britain's vulnerability from the air which made it necessary for the main work to be done in America but Britain's want of physical resources.

If Britain after the war were to raise the general standard of living and create more wealth to do so it seemed logical that she would have to control her material and manpower resources far more precisely than in the past. America could afford lavish waste and marauding capitalists. America could afford gigantic mistakes. America did not have to be certain of selling a huge proportion of her output overseas to survive. Exports for America were the jam on top, not the very bread of her existence as they were for Britain.

It could not be expected, it seemed to me, that in Britain everything could be left to chance and the haphazard workings of the free enterprise system. Very considerable and exact planning from the central government would be essential to make the best use of what we had. This was not a doctrinaire approach, a desire for direction for its own sake. It was a pragmatic necessity, but naturally it could not be achieved in a democracy unless people at all levels were willing to make it work. If greed were their only motive there would not be much hope.

The war, and the behaviour of those in and out of the Forces, suggested that there was a genuine and lasting spirit of sacrifice, and a determination to do all for the common good, which could be built upon. If the Army could be run decently and without thought of private profit in peacetime as well as in war why not the rest of the nation?

When everyone saw how little we had and how much we wanted and needed to do with it surely common sense would dictate that equality of opportunity and the fair distribution of national wealth should prevail?

After everyone had more or less shared equally in the struggle to stay free it seemed unthinkable that there should be a return to uncontrolled free enterprise which would be certain to misuse our resources. There could be few, I thought, who would wish to put private property and individual wealth ahead of the survival of the nation.

So ideals seemed to merge with practicality. The people would not try to help the nation to make the best use of its resources and to export enough to make itself richer unless the worst cases of prewar injustice were removed. If only a few were to be the happy beneficiaries of Britain's ability to survive and advance then the right national will and the necessary efforts would not be present. And if wealth were not increased, or maintained, there could not be much lessening of social injustice by its redistribution. Planning and ideals marched together, it seemed. The war, I believed, had proved that self-interest was much less important as a motive force than had been supposed. People would expect some differential for higher skills and harder work but would not be galvanized only by the hope of becoming extremely rich.

The controls and direction required to implement this planning would not be inimical to individual freedom, I supposed. That was because they would be operated with general consent. Since the intention was reasonable and the results of the planning would uplift the multitude without dragging down managers, valuable entrepreneurs and skilled practitioners in the professions there could be little

18

dissent. Some would grumble but without public approval. Controls arising from the planning would restrain only those whose activities were manifestly damaging to the community. Restrictions on individual liberty would be no worse in application than those rules which must always regulate groups of people living together.

To prevent a man driving at more than thirty miles an hour is an infringement of his liberty. So is the law which says that he must not spend all his income or dispose of all his property freely upon his death but must give a proportion of it to the State. A right of way is a liberty in the eyes of the walker but a curtailment of it to the farmer who is thereby prevented from keeping a bull in his field. To be privately drunk is to exercise an individual choice: to be publicly drunk, insulting and violent is to act in a way which annoys other individuals and is therefore prohibited if there are enough police around.

There was never any difficulty in Britain in understanding that there must be prescribed limits to the freedom of each individual if the exercise of that freedom harmed or reduced the liberties of others. The Social Democracy envisaged by my contemporaries was a natural progression in the British tradition. The Factory Acts had restricted the freedom of employers to use child labour, even when that child labour was voluntarily offered, and nobody thought that this was a blow against democracy. Attempts to strike a reasonable balance between individual rights and the common good have always been extended as the interaction of people's activities upon each other have grown more complicated in modern living.

Our Social Democracy had no connection with the suppression of free speech or criticism. We did not aim to prevent the creation of wealth or to stop people making themselves rich by it provided the wealth creation helped the community at large and a reasonable tax was paid upon it. We did not aim to abolish public schools or prevent the middle classes sending their children to universities. We wished to make the best education available to all who could profit from it. There was much virtue in the middle-class way of life with its strong morality and cultural aspirations

19

which had produced so much that was good and admirable in Britain. But it is difficult to enjoy, appreciate and multiply the benefits of the middle-class ethos without middle-class conditions to live in.

I saw Social Democracy as a way of giving the same fullness of life to the great mass of people that our economic maladministration had broadly permitted only to the middle classes and above. There was nothing wrong with gracious living except that too few were able to live graciously.

As being middle class was pleasant, how desirable it was for everybody to be middle class. Middle-class standards were the product of centuries of the civilizing process. Neither the middle classes nor their way of life were to be torn down to make way for a drab proletariat. It was the drab proletariat whose lives were to be enriched.

CHAPTER TWO

General Acceptance of the Social Democratic Revolution

FROM ATTLEE'S *As It Happened* or *A Prime Minister Remembers* (in which Lord Attlee is interviewed by Francis Williams) it can be judged that Attlee's views and outlook were formed in the same way as the views of those of a similar background to his in my generation were formed in the Second World War. But by 1935–45 there were more of us who were susceptible to a conversion to Socialism than there were in 1914–18.

Attlee was a pioneer who had shaped his approach to Social Democracy before the First World War when he worked in the East End of London for a boys' club maintained by his old public school, Haileybury. In 1907 he took over as club manager and actually lived in the East End for fourteen years apart from his Army service in the First World War.

He hoped for future progress through the merging of the classes, not their polarization into bitter enmity. Classlessness was his aim and it was not through chance that he should have tried to help the disadvantaged in the East End from a base erected by his old public school to which he remained ever devoted. It must have been puzzling to Attlee before the last war to have been considered by most of the middle classes as a dangerous revolutionary since his aim was to extend to everyone the merits and fullness of the way they lived and flourished.

Attlee's ideas were simple. Laconic and unimaginative, he did not express them excitingly and could not inspire great audiences to enthusiasm nor did he wrap his ideas in intellectual sophistry capable of fascinating the intelligentsia. Consequently the importance of the two books I have mentioned, in understanding what his Labour Government of 1945 was all about and what Social Democracy is, has been underestimated.

But his plainness and simplicity of intention were considerable assets in promoting enormous change. Only someone with his straightforward patriotism, practical desire to do practical good, and proclaimed belief in the middle-class virtues could have persuaded the middle classes to acquiesce in, and cooperate with, the plans of the 1945–51 Labour Government. He was the guarantee that whatever might be said about a revolution taking place it would not be a revolution in terms of a Left Wing dictatorship so long as he was Prime Minister, and that such a revolution was not contemplated. Nor was it a revolution in the sense of overturning the structure of society or of violently replacing one set of leaders of society by another. It was more the making of profound changes by a logical continuation of tendencies which were already quite visible and which had a long history in Britain.

There was nothing new, for instance, in the idea of nationalizing the mines. Lord Sankey's Commission (Lord Sankey was from 1929–1935 Lord Chancellor) had recommended much the same in 1919. It was commonly agreed that most mine owners through their folly had settled upon the workforce a sullen resentment from which higher productivity or even cooperation could never emerge. It had also been long accepted that it was an affront that many mine owners should be unusually rich by the mere chance of having coal seams under their land. Indeed coal royalties had already been nationalized in 1938.

Coal was a basic necessity. It did not demand much commercial skill in marketing nor was there great scope for inventing new types of coal. The profit motive could not be, or seemed not to be, important in determining the price or quality of coal but with industry still running primarily on coal, or its by-products, the provision of coal was a public service without which it would be impossible to exist. When challenged to have a stronger foreign policy Ernest Bevin used to reply that if he was given fifty million tons more coal to export he would have one. Without nationalization even the home supply of this basic commodity would be jeopardized.

Much the same could be said about electricity and gas. Like water, which strangely was in large part not, and is still not, nationalized, they were public utilities. It is conceivable that had they not been nationalized competition might have made them more efficient but the waste of resources would have been substantial. Two lots of electricity companies laying cables in the same street in an attempt to get custom away from each other would hardly have been worth the effort. Apportioning regions to different private electricity companies would have created local monopolies little different from centralized nationalization.

The Conservatives had themselves created the Central Electricity Board in 1926. This owned the National Grid sending electricity all over the country. Over half the generating stations were already municipally owned so that the State owning and controlling the whole electricity service was not a notion alarming or unfamiliar to Conservatives.

Civil aviation may have been a more doubtful case but many free enterprise countries nationalize their civil aviation, or subsidize it to such an extent that it might just as well be nationalized. If a service is essential but not necessarily profitable it has to be kept going by subsidy or nationalization.

Moreover British civil aviation could not operate in a vacuum. The pride of every other country demanding that each should run its own airline ensured that British civil aviation would have competitors.

In 1940 the Coalition Government had set up British Overseas Airways as a public corporation. Churchill's 'Caretaker' Government of 1945 intended three corporations for aviation. They would have been under a mixture of public and private ownership. For civil aviation to be in the main publicly owned was not a novel departure, particularly as private airlines were allowed to exist though the publicly owned corporations had a monopoly of scheduled routes.

23

As for the railways nobody wanted to own them privately. They would have all shut down long before without government subsidies, though they could argue that had they not been required to run passenger and goods services on unprofitable lines as a public service they might have made a profit. Nevertheless, the railways were still part of the infrastructure which could not be dispensed with. Modernization and increased efficiency could only come about through government intervention not through hope of profit.

Nationalization of the Bank of England did two things. It satisfied the Labour Party's desire for revenge against the financial institutions which they believed had brought down the 1931 Government, and it regularized a relationship. There did not seem very much argument against the central bank of a country being controlled by its Government. For the two to work against each other would be absurd. And as the Bank of England, broadly speaking, could only make profits out of its transactions arising out of its State connection, there seemed no strong reasons why these should be private profits. In the event, the Governor of the Bank of England and his Court of Directors were left with more than nominal independence and with a freedom of expression which has been used, and not sparingly. Possibly the relations between the Governor of the Bank of England and the Government would have been no different today if the Bank had never been nationalized. Though it could now be desirable to give the Bank some independent right to control the money supply and, hence inflation.

Few even amongst the warmest admirers of nationalization supposed that the nationalized industries would make much profit. They were charged only with breaking even, taking one year with another – a formula which no one understood then or has understood since. The important point was that the basic industries necessary to keep the rest of industry going should be in public ownership. The range of public control would thus be enlarged and the ability of the Government to influence economic events for the good of all would be enhanced.

This all seemed conventional and understandable Social

24

Democracy, though in retrospect it seems less of a conscious and well thought out plan than the kind of action which in the main any Government might have tended towards taking. Still it was a *sine qua non* for building a Social Democratic State.

In tandem with nationlization came the National Insurance Act providing improved pensions and social-security benefits for all. This Act, too, was not revolutionary as it largely stemmed from the Beveridge Report commissioned by the wartime Coalition Government. It removed major social injustices but not in an unexpected manner since it was a natural consequence of what had been agreed in the Coalition Government. Indeed, the Family Allowance Act had actually been passed into law by Churchill's Caretaker Government, which filled the space between the end of the Coalition and the general election, and the Act was in itself an important part of the new social-security arrangements. The Butler Education Act of 1944, to which the Labour Government were the willing heirs, was passed by the Coalition Government. It remains the basis of the postwar reform of the educational system.

The introduction of the National Health Service met some indignant resistance. This was partly because the doctors found Nye Bevan, Minister of Health, provocative and the doctors themselves were unimaginative and fearful of losing money and status. There were also some genuine doubts as to whether the National Health Service would unreasonably interfere with individual liberty. But the Act passed and the collection of measures of which it was a part became known as the Welfare State.

Taken separately each piece of nationalization and each piece of legislation creating the Welfare State was not revolutionary. But the total package did signify a very real change. It was undoubtedly a shift away from the hope that individuals pursuing their own interests would un-intentionally but inevitably create the common good, to the belief that large-scale State planning was needed to achieve it. The whole, once its separate parts were assembled, had quite a different aspect from the several parts taken one by one. It was the appearance of the whole which aroused the strongest opposition amongst Conservatives and which drew the greatest support from the public at large.

The public had not voted to create Social Democracy as I and others like me had. They, as the decisive vote in that part of the electorate which changes sides always does, had voted against the Government in power. In this instance the Conservatives collected the odium of having been in power when the war came upon us, of the prewar unemployment which full employment created by arms production during the war had seemed to prove avoidable and of all the dislikes attaching to a ruling Party after fourteen years.

Nevertheless the public, including the middle classes, were either pleased or disarmed by Attlee's journey into Social Democracy. So much so that R. A. Butler saw that advertising an intention to break it up would be disastrous to Conservative electoral chances. Far wiser to accept what had been done and offer to make it work better. Thus Attlee went a long way towards converting the majority of the Conservative Party to an irreversible and substantial element of Social Democracy because his character and demeanour had already converted the majority of their followers.

In the early years of the Atlee Government the mood of selflessness which had emerged during the war remained powerful. Only the stupid could have expected an immediate end to rationing and controls. The rationing was used by the Labour Government to continue to hold general living standards above a mere subsistence level particularly for children. Hence, for example, free and subsidized school meals which are still provided today.

The controls left over from the war were very useful to the Social Democratic purpose. Essential house and factory building had priority over luxury. The raw materials were directed to those who would export with them. Sir Stafford Cripps was able to compel the motor-car manufacturers to export a very high percentage of their output or be deprived of steel to make any motor cars at all. This he did against the protests of the motor-car manufacturers who said they would be unable to compete in foreign markets unless they had big home sales as a base (but they exported much better then without a big home base than today, though it must be admitted they had no competition from outside America).

Important in the attack on the worst injustices was redistribution of wealth. It was possible to levy higher taxes on middle and top earners without uproar because the process had begun during the war. Further attacks on inherited wealth or large blocks of capital were accepted without much fight because the general public were not personally affected by them and because there was an acceptance that wealth had been unevenly distributed beyond reason and the bounds of rough fairness.

But apart from steel, no serious threats had been made against significant sections of free enterprise. The Labour Government of 1945 were convinced that prosperity could not be increased unless free enterprise was strong. The Labour manifesto of 1950 said 'Labour's aim is to give a fair chance to everybody in industry, above all to the smaller concerns which have been the most ruthlessly exploited by trusts, cartels and rings. The less efficient firms will be helped to raise themselves to the standard of the best.'

It is true that the same manifesto proposed nationalization of cement, sugar, the chemical industry and water. But from the tone of the manifesto it was clear that Attlee and his Social Democratic colleagues did not think in terms of huge additions of vast industry to the nationalization programme. The nationalization of steel had already been put into the legislative process. If they had believed that Britain should basically cease to be a free enterprise country they would have planned, for their hoped-for second five years, a nationalization programme on the scale of their first five years.

The worst that free enterprise was threatened with in the manifesto of 1950 was: 'But where private enterprise fails to meet the public interest the Government will be empowered to start new competitive public enterprises in appropriate circumstances. For private and public enterprise to compete fairly and squarely in the public interest will be good for both.'

It was clear that the leaders of the Labour Party were satisfied that the mixture was now about right. If the nationalization of steel had not been a public commitment in the 1945 manifesto they would have been happy to have excluded that from nationalization. They very nearly did. A compromise suggestion from the British Iron and Steel Federation that steel should be governed by an Iron and Steel Board with considerable powers over the industry was almost accepted.

The reluctance with which nationalization of steel was carried through indicated that the principal authors of the postwar Social Democratic revolution were satisfied that the Government did not need much more public ownership to enable them to rectify major injustices. Through the Treasury, and the State departments connected with the economy, the Government could and did wield enormous influence over industry.

The Government did not have to acquire great industries to ensure that the money and resources were available for welfare service. That could be, and was, done by taxation. Equality of opportunity had spread prodigiously. The boy or girl who wanted to go to university could get there however poor their family provided they had the ability. The percentage of State-aided undergraduates at Oxford and Cambridge rose rapidly from the prewar figure of around twenty per cent to eighty per cent. (Today almost every university student is State-aided.) Potential university entrants were not driven to leave school at fourteen because full employment had raised the level of prosperity and their earnings were not essential to family survival.

Medical and dental care were universally provided. Good housing was not yet available to all. But that was nothing to do with the private ownership of building firms. It was a matter of logistics. Obsolescent and obsolete housing could not be replaced in less than some twenty years. Nor was it possible to make new hospitals spring up overnight whatever the extent of public ownership.

The social ethos had been changed. No one any longer disputed that merit rather than background should be the criterion for entry into the Civil Service or into the commissioned ranks of the armed services. It was now possible for the meritorious to win their deserts.

It was at this point that the divisions in the Labour Party began to be more noticeable. All could unite in what had been done so far. They could not unite in thinking that little more needed to be done by way of public ownership, and the restraint of private individuals in their personal pursuit of wealth, to improve the environment in which major injustices could be permanently removed and progress continued towards a juster, if not the just, society.

Nearly all those who voted Labour were satisfied. So were the majority of the Parliamentary Labour Party, of trade unionists and of trade-union leaders. But there were many in the Labour Party who were not.

CHAPTER THREE

Only Ginger Groups still want more Ginger

T H E   G R E A T Divide in the Labour Party was there from the very beginning of the 1945 Parliament. It was obscured but not obliterated by the unhesitating support of the Labour Party inside and outside the House of Commons for the programme which the Attlee Government set about carrying through. There was considerable confidence in the ability and intentions of the leaders of the Labour Party.

This did not prevent criticisms of what some thought was the slowness with which the Government proceeded. Very young myself, I shared that impatience. I allowed very little for delays inevitably arising in administration and caused by shortage of Parliamentary time preventing immediate passage of all the necessary legislation. Nor did I make much allowance for the financial and economic difficulties left behind by the war. The bright and enthusiastic, for example, thought that pensions should have been increased faster and by more. I was rebuked by Atlee for demanding that the troops should be demobilized faster because he thought that I, as an ex-major, ought to have known that it was not practical.

But such impatience was directed at a quicker removal of the most serious injustices. It did not go to the heart of the Divide. That argument as it developed concerned means and ends. Those who shared my approach appraised each act of public ownership or direction over the activities of the individual for its value in contributing towards the erection of the just society. We did not think of them as ends in themselves as others, still very much in the minority, did.

For some, public ownership was a good end in itself. They

would have advocated the extension of State ownership even if they had been convinced, which they were not, that it would lead to lower productivity and less prosperity.

The very ownership by the State of large chunks of industry employing millions seemed desirable to them. It broke the power of the capitalist enemy. That it also increased the power of the State and the power of the politicians who sat in the offices of State was not considered a drawback. The motives of Socialists could only be good. They were immune from the cravings of power which beset impure mortals.

The boundary of the Great Divide was blurred. The same people were not always on the same side of it in every issue. Many, including myself, had but the dimmest awareness that there was such a divide.

But the signs were there. In November 1946 R.H.S. Crossman put down an amendment to the King's Speech demanding that the Government 'Re-cast its conduct of international affairs'. It was supported by fifty-seven Labour M.P.s. Some of them were genuine Social Democrats. Many of the rest were soon to be arguing that neither the Government nor the Labour Party were Socialist enough at home: the Social Democratic society of Attlee and his senior colleagues was very far short of the red-blooded Socialism they wanted. Those who were crypto-Communists in the Parliamentary Labour Party naturally were included among the signatories of the Crossman amendment.

In April 1948 came the Nenni telegram. It was signed by thirty-seven Labour M.P.s and it wished Nenni, leader of the Italian Socialist Party cooperating with the Communist Party, good luck in the Italian general elections. The Italian Saragat Social Democrats were ignored. At that time the leaders of the Labour Party were still confident in their ascendancy. The organizer of the telegram, John Platts-Mills, was expelled from the Labour Party. Sixteen Labour M.P.s who had signed the telegram rapidly retracted. The twenty-one who refused to do so were given a week to climb down or face expulsion along with Platts-Mills. They obeyed.

31

In the same year two more Labour M.P.s were expelled, Konni Zilliacus and L. J. Solley. Their crime was to extol the virtues of the Russian Communist puppet governments in Eastern Europe. They were not even allowed to defend themselves at the Labour Party conference.

In 1949 another Labour M.P., Lester Hutchinson, was expelled for persistent criticism of Ernest Bevin's foreign policy. His criticisms were directed from a distinctly Communist angle. This strict disciplining, either by a caution or by expulsion of a group of Labour M.P.s, could be put down to a lack of tolerance then prevailing in the Parliamentary Labour Party.

That would be a wrong deduction. It happened because the Social Democrats were in complete control. Flirting with Marxism, beyond taking an interest in Marxist economic theories, was abhorrent to them. They could not agree that kind words about Communist states was consistent with membership of the Labour Party.

In that atmosphere of solid Social Democracy expulsions raised no problem. It is the clearest possible indication of the change of outlook which has come over the Labour Party since the 1945-51 period. No Labour leader today would dare suggest expelling Labour M.P.s expressing the views of Platts-Mills, Konni Zilliacus, L. J. Solley and Lester Hutchinson. Then the suggestion that a Trotskyist should be appointed as a whole-time official at Labour Party headquarters would never have survived incredulous laughter. In 1977 the actual appointment could not be prevented even by a Labour Prime Minister.

In May 1947 fifteen Labour M.P.s published a pamphlet called *Keep Left*. The prime authors were R. H. S. Crossman, Michael Foot and Ian Mikardo though all fifteen collaborated. I wrote most of the passage on demobilization and defence. At the time *Keep Left* was regarded as a note of Left Wing dissent from the Labour Government, much resented in official and orthodox circles.

How mild it seems today.

There were pages of praise for the achievements of the new Labour Government. The new fairness was enthusiastically welcomed. A telling example was given. Milk rationing was still in force in 1947, limiting each person to two pints a week. Before the war, it was pointed out, Britain consumed 767 million gallons a year. At the beginning of 1947 the annual total was 1,132 million gallons a year.

'How', asked the pamphlet, 'is it that many of us feel that we are short of milk at a time when the country as a whole is consuming nearly fifty per cent more? The answer is that before the war the people of such places as Wallsend and Jarrow consumed on the average only one-tenth of a pint a day. They could not afford any more: they were rationed by poverty. Today, under Labour rule, they are getting two pints a week like everyone else. Milk is certainly a 'first thing". Labour has put it first.'

We had little quarrel with the general trend of the Labour Government's activities. The improvements in the social services were commended – the new sickness and unemployment benefits, family allowances, the increased old-age pensions, better pensions for disabled ex-servicemen. The raising of the school-leaving age, the housing drive were praised. The National Health Service due to start in 1948 was eagerly awaited. Approval was recorded for the benefits derived from nationalizing coal and electricity.

In the passage on demobilization my concern was not that the Government were deliberately delaying demobilization but that the plan to reduce the armed forces by 340,000 by March 1948 could be improved upon. I contended that a reduction of another 300,000 was possible if the right effort were made. That would still have left us with 800,000 men in the Services – over 450,000 more than we had in 1977. The main reason that demobilization was so slow was the new insistence on absolute fairness. First in, first out, was the rule. Servicemen could not be demobilized in blocks when it was convenient: scattered all over the globe, they had to be sifted through on a length-of-service basis.

The emphasis was largely on greater speed in fulfilling the Government's declared objectives. 'The main theme running right through this book is that we need, in all our plans, a greater sense of *urgency* than has been shown over the last couple of years, and a realization that the economic struggle we have got on our hands can't be waged with the leisureliness of a phoney war.'

The Government were given twenty things to do *now*. Impracticably (to save hard currency) luxury food imports were to be curtailed and tobacco was to be rationed. At the time strong arguments were being advanced that foreign workers should be brought in or allowed, if already here, to make up the labour shortage in the mines and other industries. The Keep Lefters were firmly against this unless the foreign workers had '"ready-made" skills which we really need e.g. foundry workers'. This xenophobia apparently did not extend to coloured immigrants when they began to arrive in large numbers. Till then the prejudice hit hardest at Poles and others dispossessed in their countries who, at the cost of all they had, had helped us during the war.

Some suggestions on the home front were sensible. Taxation 'on both wages and profits in the essential industries' was to be lowered. This incentive for employees is still not here in 1977. Thirty years ahead of the Bullock Committee we proposed the compulsory establishment in industry of joint production committees with definite powers. Not at all a bad idea. If it had been implemented it might have led to a gradual and organic increase in employee participation. There would have been greater understanding between management and employees, fewer strikes, higher output and a more rational appreciation of the part which could be eventually and usefully played by employee directors (if a real need for them were proved).

The Eastern European countries were not regarded, by most of us, as havens of commendable Socialism. There should be 'forms of European collaboration designed gradually to remove the Iron Curtain'. Elections in Eastern Europe were described as a farce.

Nevertheless, there were glimpses of the cloven hoof. The Government were exhorted to renounce the manufacture of atomic bombs. Why I agreed to this I cannot now remember. It must have been from a touching belief that the world was about to reform itself. The Government were also told to renounce 'staff conversations with non-European powers'. This was directed against military collaboration with the U.S.A. while disingenuously protesting friendship with America.

President Truman's proposals for collective security against Communism were to be repudiated. Britain, according to us, was to be some kind of an intermediate or third force, cooperating with France while working for a united but militarily impotent Germany. There was a tendency to equate American policy with Russian. The pamphlet did not go quite so far as to say that the Americans were as bad as the Russians but it drifted in that direction.

The pamphlet argued that we should be friends and not satellites of America, maintaining an equal influence in the world with the U.S.A. We were to 'Oppose Communism not by allying ourselves with reactionary forces, but by helping to put something better in its place'.

The twentieth job the Government had to do *now* was 'Seize the opportunity for leadership in the United Nations which a Socialist Britain is offered. – The world wants neither Russian nor American domination. Recognize our own strength and use it wisely to tip the balance against war and lead the way to world government through really United Nations.'

Heady stuff which ignored the wise advice given elsewhere in the pamphlet that we should recognize that we were no longer a great power. But, taken as a whole, *Keep Left* was not very Left. This might have been expected from a group which contained five future life peers and eight future more or less respectable Labour Ministers. Possibly the worst of its propositions was that we should not take 'sides either in a Communist bloc or in an anti-Bolshevik axis' as though there were not much to choose between the two.

I cannot believe I really thought like this in 1947 but if I did I must plead that I was not yet twenty-nine and considerably inferior in intellect and political argument to some of my associates. Nor, with many others in the new Parliamentary Labour Party, had I yet woken up to the dangers of Soviet imperialism. Churchill's Fulton speech

35

had not long been made and he and Ernest Bevin were regarded as very Right Wing figures, too old to understand that the Russian Communists meant no harm and would by some unspecified alchemy slowly turn democratic. In 1947 it was not at all incompatible with Social Democracy to think that a genuine cooperation between the Soviet Union and the West was possible. The signing of the *Keep Left* pamphlet did not carry with it to all the signatories the connotation of fellow-travelling or an acceptance of Marxism.

So, the very Left were still impotent. Instances here and there indicated their presence but not alarmingly. However, there was an insistence on the nationalization of steel which went beyond the assumption that this would be good for the economy. You could not be 'Socialist' unless you backed it. Morrison and others with second thoughts on steel in the Cabinet were labelled as Right Wing. Sir Stafford Cripps, to whom I was close, fell under suspicion of leaning towards this heresy because he had not said much openly in favour of the nationalization of steel. I remember prompting him to include a strong passage in that vein in one of his major economic speeches in the Commons. I did not want my hero to be accused of resiling from 'Socialism'.

Words and names have great importance. I suppose an early Christian who advocated keeping some of the old gods, rituals, superstitions and customs was likely to be suspected of not being a true Christian though the Christian Churches did incorporate many of them. A burning faith had to be demonstrated. Doubts on so big a question as steel implied that there might be doubts on other serious matters.

Maybe it was over steel that the cleavage began to manifest itself. As the private steel companies began to show increasing willingness to be subject to Government policy direction and to submit their siting and expansion plans for approval, provided they were allowed to keep their day-to-day management and operate for a profit on commercial lines, the nationalization of steel became less pragmatic and more dogmatic.

Twelve Labour M.P.s published a further pamphlet *Keeping Left* in January 1950. By this time I was not of their number. Though *Keeping Left* was not very adventurous it went a little further in spirit than *Keep Left*. There was nothing yet for Attlee and the leading Social Democrats to be much alarmed about.

CHAPTER FOUR

Marxists and Friends begin to Profit from Disaffection

ATTLEE'S 1945 Government seemed to have established a permanent pattern of Social Democracy. With some reluctance they had legislated to nationalize steel (the Act was repealed, before it came into force, by the 1951–5 Conservative Government) but there was scant enthusiasm for going much further down the public ownership road. There was a general view in the Parliamentary Labour Party that the mixture of free enterprise and public ownership was approximately right. There was no point in large-scale essays into nationalization unless they could be justified on the grounds that they would increase productivity and profits for the nation. What was needed was consolidation.

It seemed sensible that industrialists and businessmen should be persuaded that Labour governments were not manned by ogres and that it was possible to make as much or more profits with them as they could with Tory governments. By the leadership of Sir Stafford Cripps the unions had been convinced that wage restraints were in the interests of their members. The process of reconciling normally anti-Socialist elements to the idea of a Social Democratic government was on its way.

A new stability in society had been created. There were many injustices remaining to be removed but the manner in which many injustices had already been removed, or mitigated, did not provoke fears that a steady progress towards greater fairness would wreck the chances of industry being able to deliver enough extra goods and so make the Social Democratic ideal of wider redistribution of wealth a bar to creating the extra wealth needed.

38

Even the prospect of the nationalization of insurance and cement had receded. Enough had been done to make a base from which the worst poverty could be eliminated and equality of opportunity could be extended. The fierceness of the desire to make men equal had subsided. This aim was recognized as impossible. But that all could be treated equally was a realizable proposition.

There was no pressing demand for any drastic upheavals. There were bastions of undeserved privilege but they could be broken or modified. It was not necessary for instance, to abolish the public schools. There was a strong feeling that they could lose their influence by being obliged to accept State-scholarship boys and girls to dilute their class outlook. Nepotism arising from inherited wealth was still prevalent in industry but under the impact of increased death duties and higher taxation it was diminishing.

In 1950 it did not seem to me that fundamental changes were still required. Nor did it seem so to those who held the power upon which Attlee's Government rested. The dissidents in the Parliamentary Labour Party were helpless. They could not appeal to the Labour Party conference over the heads of the Parliamentary leadership. The Party conferences were overwhelming in their loyalty to Attlee and his Cabinet. The block votes were controlled by the union leaders and the union leaders were content with what had been done and did not want any more crusading 'Socialism'.

There was a solid look about the Labour Government and the Labour Party. They had proved purposeful but moderate. The Conservatives had not been greatly outraged by their actions. Their main annoyance was that they no longer had power. The Marxist element in the Labour Party still had little influence. The passion for ever more nationalization and Government direction, though present, was not yet taken seriously.

In my election address at Aston, Birmingham, for the February 1950 election I did not mention nationalization once. I rested, as did most other Labour candidates, on the record of the Labour Government. I assumed that the Labour Government had been able to do so much because it had been supported by the continuation of the general desire to serve the common good prompted by the war.

'I want to thank you,' I wrote, 'for the wonderful way in which, whatever your political faith may be, you have supported the Labour Government during the last four and a half years. It is because you, and millions like you, have responded to the Government's appeals for higher production, and because you have understood why it was not possible to have everything we wanted immediately after the war, that Britain has come so successfully through the difficulties that the war caused and left behind.'

I summed up the great social transformation not in revolutionary terms but by saying, 'Now Britain is run in the interests of the many and not mainly in the interests of the privileged and well-to-do few. That is what the Tories don't like.

'Just think back to the days before the war for the moment. Aren't ordinary people better off now than they were, in spite of all the shortages in the world?'

It was very simple stuff but it was the right mood. On the back of my election address I listed a number of Labour achievements. Not only did I make no reference to nationalization in the future but the acts of nationalization which had taken place were not considered sufficiently important to be listed or referred to. The increase in old-age pensions, the introduction of family allowances and the free health service were far more significant than Labour's intention to complete the nationalization of steel which I did not mention at all. Full employment and the rise in the standard of living and the exemption of four million people from paying income tax featured in my election address as having more meaning than theoretical notions about Socialism.

I do not think I was out of touch with broad national feeling. So what did I see as the future of the Labour Party at that time? If it were not going to advance to the State ownership of everything which mattered and to equality of income for everyone, what was it to do?

As I saw it, its task was to improve the quality of life by consistently diverting enough resources into good housing, good education, good amenities, good medical care, good pensions. As for pensions, I did not see the State going so far as to penalize the thrifty or the enterprising by reducing the benefits given by the State to the individual according to the extent to which he had provided for himself, thus curbing incentives. Along with such agreeable aims went the belief that equality of opportunity would have to be worked at for many years before it could be said to have a truly general application. It would be a long time before we got to the classless society but it would be an excellent thing to get there.

As late as 1956 in *The Future of Socialism* Anthony Crosland recorded the enormous advance made towards greater fairness in the distribution of wealth by progressive taxation. As he said, 'When every allowance is made, the essential fact remains – that the rich are distinctly less rich, and the poor much less poor. The levelling process is more a reality even in terms of consumption after six years of Labour rule either than it was before the war, or than it otherwise would have been.'

All this had nothing to do with nationalization. It had very little to do with the way in which industry was to be organized. The trend had been set for it to make sufficient profits to pay for social advances. The argument between the main body of the Labour Party and the Conservative Party at that time was mainly how much social welfare was to be provided by the Government and how far it was reasonable to pay for it by increased taxation, not whether industry was correctly structured to create the necessary wealth.

There was no merit in dispossessing capitalists just because they were capitalists. This should only be done if they were inefficient capitalists and not initiating the creation of as much wealth as could reasonably be expected. Nor was there any appeal in the idea of taking incentives away from them to perform this necessary function.

The Attlee Labour Government left the broad consensus of opinion within and outside the Labour Party that Britain was very much a mixed economy and that sufficient had been done in extending the area of direct State ownership.

41

Of course, apart from public schools, disliked for their privilege, there was dispute about the educational system. Social Democrats tended to believe in the comprehensive school. The eleven-plus examination seemed altogether unfair in making selection at so early an age. Hence the Social Democratic desire for the comprehensive school.

Tories stuck to public schools and grammar schools as being the only way in which the community could rely on finding renewed supplies of leaders. What Social Democrats called elitism they called a healthy stimulus to ambition both among parents and children.

Tories were naturally convinced that high incomes were being taxed too heavily though now they conceded that before the war they had been taxed too gently. They considered that there was something wrong in the way in which the nationalized industries were run though they didn't know what, or what to do about it. Aside from steel, finally nationalized before the 1951 election, and which they denationalized, they proposed to leave the nationalized industries alone. Disagreements between the two main parties officially were not fundamental. They amounted more to a matter of how much emphasis should be given to nourishing the Welfare State rather than to any proposals to dismantle it.

The electorate would have settled for this Tweedledum and Tweedledee approach. The union leaders were well satisfied with the improved living standards and status won by their members. There was every prospect of Britain proceeding indefinitely on a Social Democratic course. I would have forecast then that in the second half of the seventies Britain would have a similar structure to that created by the West German Social Democratic Government. Hence it would not matter greatly whether the Labour or the Conservative Party won general elections.

This could have happened, and Britain would have been a much healthier and more united country, but for two things. One was the absence of a Communist Party able to win seats in Parliament. The other was an unfortunate breakdown in civilized relations between leading figures in the Labour Party.

42

In 1950 all the Communist Party's 100 candidates were defeated, including the two Communist M.P.s who had sat in the 1945 Parliament. This heightened the determination of the Communists to control the Labour Party by indirect means since they could not establish themselves in Parliament under their own name. Already the Communists had been for some years the masters of the Electricians' Union by rigging the ballots. This gave them a minor say at Labour Party conferences. They now concentrated on capturing the important Engineers' Union either through open Communists or through those who for tactical or other reasons did not disclose themselves as Communist sympathizers.

Some of the extremists in the Parliamentary Labour Party since 1945 were actually undercover Communists, others were very close to the Communist viewpoint. In France or Italy such people would have been happy to declare themselves Communists and would have had a reasonable chance of becoming M.P.s. It was the general hostility towards Communists in Britain which drove them to dissemble. If a candidate in a general election was known to be a Communist he had no chance of success whatever. But how was the electorate, whether Parliamentary or union, to know that a candidate they were invited to vote for was not genuinely an orthodox Social Democrat member of the Labour Party when he said he was?

The secret Communist, or Communist-inclined, M.P.s naturally supported any group which disagreed with Attlee-style orthodoxy. They encouraged such groups to believe that they were the true Socialists and that the leaders of the Labour Party and the unions served the interests of capitalists more than Socialism. This was very flattering to those who liked to consider themselves as real redblooded Socialists who understood Marxism while protesting that they did not favour the totalitarian regime without which Marxism cannot be applied.

The importance of deception to the Communists can be seen by their fury when a low-profile Communist is publicly identified as such. In union elections in particular, Communist candidates react furiously to being called

Communists on the grounds that this is witch-hunting and outside interference. They know very well that so long as voters are not aware that candidates are Communists, or fellow-travellers, many will vote for them who otherwise would not.

This absence of an openly successful Communist Party led to an infiltration of the Labour Party which was difficult to identify. There was no clear line between total Communists and those who shaded off towards Social Democracy.

In 1950 the danger did not seem considerable. Though the genuine Social Democrats like R. H. S. Crossman were happy to get the support of Communists and near Communists in rebellions against the orthodox leadership, the leaders of the rebellions, though they were a nuisance, were not powerful enough to disturb the hold that Attlee and his colleagues had in the Parliamentary Labour Party and in the trade unions.

A change came with the resignation of Sir Stafford Cripps. Rivalries and jealousies which smouldered until then burst out with his going. Nye Bevan thought that he was the natural successor as Chancellor of the Exchequer to Cripps. It was an important stage in his ambition to become Leader of the Labour Party. Instead he was made Minister of Labour and the Ministry of Health from which he had created the National Health Service was demoted in rank so that its Minister was no longer in the Cabinet. It was clear that an explosion would not be long in coming. To understand why, the nature of Labour politicians must be understood.

In the Labour Party a great deal is said about loyalty. But the word is not used with the meaning normally attached to it in ordinary life. Whatever Labour politicians may admit to in their secret moments publicly they maintain that they are in the Labour Party not for hope of personal advancement but to serve the cause. Their much trumpeted loyalty is to the Labour Movement, not to individuals. Joe Haines could justify writing his book about Sir Harold Wilson's Kitchen Cabinet because of his alleged duty to be loyal to the Labour Movement. That loyalty wiped out any considerations of personal loyalty to the Leader of the Labour Party who hired him as his Press Officer. As I have already said, the Labour Party is not an ordinary political party but is more a religion.

Nye Bevan was particularly hypocritical in denouncing people who talked of personalities instead of policies in connection with the Labour Party. But he was not alone in that. Treachery, it was claimed, could never be to persons but only to ideals. Everyone is, or can be, his own judge of ideals and policies. It is easy to say that you are attacking the leadership not because you want their jobs but because they are straying from virtue. To point out that personal gain would follow a successful attack was considered indecent. Normal considerations of personal honour generally do not apply in the Labour Party.

Until recently Conservatives defeated for the leadership or disappointed at not getting or at being relieved of office reacted in a traditionally sportsmanlike manner. Sir Alec Douglas-Home (now Lord Home), for example, did not hesitate to serve under Edward Heath. He did not try to pull the edifice down because he was no longer on the top of it.

One reason for the lower rate of bitterness in the Conservative Party used to be that most Conservative politicans had other resources. They could return to their businesses or find businesses willing to take them on. They could go back to their estates. The Conservative politician did not depend on success in politics for his feeling of well-being to anything like the same extent as the Labour politician. Disappointment consequently did not make him nearly so frenetic. Nor did the Conservative politician feel that he was taking part in a religion which had strong absolute values outside the purely pragmatic and political consideration of forming and maintaining a workmanlike government. At least any such values were not so strong as to justify denouncing as heretics those who differed with his view of the principles of Conservatism.

The religious aspect of the Labour Party includes the proposition that the rules of human nature are suspended when Socialism reigns. Indeed, it is a part of the faith that in a truly Socialist State motivation by self-interest would cease and be replaced by a general subscription to the common good. That this has so far not happened even in the Labour Party, where intrigues directed at self-advancement are commonplace, is ignored.

Personal motivation in the Labour Party is the more dangerous because it is always camouflaged by something else to make it respectable. Partly because he has nowhere else to go and partly because he is genuinely full of confused religious notions the Labour politician out of favour or over the top will not give up what is his whole life to him. Comradeship in the usual sense is superseded ostensibly by the higher claim of dedication to the true religion.

Accordingly Nye Bevan in April 1951 did not say that he was resigning because he could not overcome his mortification at Gaitskell being Chancellor of the Exchequer. He had to dress it up, probably convincing himself that he did so as a matter of principle. Most Conservative politicians would have controlled themselves and hoped for a better turn to their fortunes in time. Rocking the boat by resignation would have made a Conservative politician vulnerable to the charge of jealousy, spite and thwarted ambition and he would have harmed himself by attacking a Government of which he had long been a member. There being no great array of articles of faith in the Conservative Party it would be pointless for a Conservative politician to try to mount an assault on the Conservative leadership under cover of a supposed betrayal of all that the Conservative Party stood for. When such an attempt has been made it has failed because no one has believed in it.

In February 1951 Nye Bevan made a very effective defence of the Labour Government's rearmament programmes introduced because of the Korean War. When he learned that Gaitskell, as Chancellor of the Exchequer, intended to introduce charges on teeth and spectacles as one of the contributions towards paying for it his anger rose to fury. Here was his precious free health service being attacked by a man he despised and whose job he thought that he should have. Imagining his position to be stronger than it was, he threatened in a speech at Bermondsey at the beginning of April that he would not remain a member of any Government which made charges in the health service. This was despite the fact that he had when Minister of Health introduced a Bill into the House of Commons to make a charge of a shilling for each prescription. For administrative reaons that measure was never implemented but it was recommended fervently to the Parliamentary Labour Party in a speech by Bevan in which he observed, 'Something has to be done about the cascades of medicine pouring down British throats and they're not even bringing the bottles back.' As numerous people remembered that speech Nye Bevan realized that he had to widen the reasons for his resignation rapidly beyond the narrow issue of teeth and spectacles. Rearmament was arousing passions among the pacifists, the Left Wing and the extremists in the Labour Party. It could be presented as an attack on Socialism because it diverted resources required for improving the Welfare State. Many sincere Social Democrats were susceptible to this argument. For the crypto-Communists and Communist-inclined it had the added attraction that it could be stigmatized as an unjust hostility to the peace-loving Soviet Union and Chinese People's Republic, from whom, they proclaimed, we had nothing to fear.

Suddenly the Left Wing had a credible leadership. Harold Wilson, then President of the Board of Trade, resigned with Nye Bevan on 23 April 1951 because he expected an adverse trade situation for which he might be blamed and because an alliance with Nye Bevan, the darling of the constituency Labour Parties, would endear him to ordinary Labour Party workers at a level he had never previously plumbed. The orthodox leadership of the Labour Party had broken ranks.

The dissenting group needed all the support they could get. They did not query the credentials of the crypto-Communists and fellow-travellers in the Parliamentary Labour Party, in the constituency parties and in the trade unions who rallied to them. The more there were behind them the more their cause would prosper. The acceptance by Bevan and Wilson of support from dubious elements made them beholden to those elements and made it more difficult to contain their influence. If the orthodox leadership of the Labour Party had remained intact the Left Wing might never have been more than a nuisance.

But now they began to pursue their aims under the flag of Bevanism as well as that of true Socialism. Many, probably most, of the Bevanites in the House of Commons were Social Democrats but they could not avoid reciprocation for the aid given them by the Marxists in their campaigns.

A tremendous impetus was given to the extremists. It was immediately reflected in the elections to the constituency section for the National Executive of the Labour Party at the Scarborough conference at the end of September 1951. It was not surprising that Bevan once again headed the list of successful candidates. He had done that for several years before he became a Bevanite.

But the orthodox leadership was shocked by Barbara Castle, long vociferous in her attacks on the Government, getting second place. Driberg (actually, as he told me, a card-carrying Communist when first elected to Parliament in 1942, though he claims in *Ruling Passions* that to his distress he was expelled just before, and who was never very far away from the Communist position until he died) won third place. Ian Mikardo, successful as an entrepreneur in trade with the Communist countries and whose views were always too extreme even for Harold Wilson to include him in a Government, came sixth.

Herbert Morrison dropped from third place to fifth.

Jim Griffiths and Hugh Dalton, also orthodox stalwarts of the Party, just managed to retain their seats but with many thousands of votes fewer than in the previous year. Shinwell, who as Minister of Defence was responsible for the rearmament programme, was pushed off the National Executive altogether. He walked out of the conference in disgust.

By the following year the extremists were really advancing, aiding the Bevanites who wanted their support in capturing the National Executive and being aided by them in turn. It was expected that Bevan would come top of the list for the constituency section of the National Executive. He did so, greatly increasing his vote.

Barbara Castle, Tom Driberg and Ian Mikardo all held their seats with higher votes. Harold Wilson and R. H. S. Crossman also won seats on the constituency section of the National Executive for the first time. The only successful candidate not an extremist or Bevanite was Jim Griffiths. Morrison and Dalton were thrown off the National Executive despite their enormous contribution to the Labour Party in the past and despite their having good years of useful service left in them. The dismissal of Morrison in favour of the extremist faction was in particular an extraordinary act. He had first joined the National Executive in 1920 and had been largely responsible for making Transport House into an effective electoral machine. He had been at the centre of drafting election manifestos and running election campaigns. He was the most experienced, lively and versatile party manager Labour ever had.

But, of course, Morrison was a reformer, not a Marxist. He believed in practical measures, not in Utopian Socialism. The Social Democrats among the Bevanites may not have known what they were doing when they destroyed him. The Marxists among their associates knew very well. Morrison was a symbol of the kind of Labour Party they hated.

Nevertheless, even in 1952 the National Executive of the Labour Party was not dominated by the extremists. As well as seven members from the constituency organizations' section there were five members from the women's section. These were solidly orthodox. The Treasurer, elected by the combined vote of the unions and constituency Parties, was Arthur Greenwood. He was a traditional reformer, not a Marxist. The twelve-strong trade-union section was almost entirely made up of orthodox loyalists. The leaders of the big unions not on the N.E.C. remained firmly behind Attlee. Arthur Deakin was still General Secretary of the Transport and General Workers' Union. Tom Williamson was General Secretary of the Municipal and General Workers' Union. Sam Watson and other orthodox Labour men like him still controlled the National Union of Mineworkers.

There was cause for uneasiness but not for despair. The management committees of the constituency Labour

Parties responsible for choosing the representatives of the constituency organizations on the National Executive had undoubtedly lurched to the populist Left. But they always had been less balanced than the rest of the Labour Movement. The Parliamentary Labour Party was still comfortably controlled by the orthodox reformers.

I was still a long way from wondering whether I was in the right political party. Nothing had cracked the Social Democratic edifice, despite a few tremors.

CHAPTER FIVE

Bevan and Wilson find useful the Support of Marxists and Extremists

THOUGH MANY Social Democratic M.P.s were worried by the trend shown in the 1951 and 1952 elections to the constituency section of the National Executive of the Labour Party, the electorate were scarcely aware that anything important had happened. They were accustomed to violent argument and vituperation in the Labour Party. Splits were easily smothered publicly as fantasies of the hostile Tory Press.

The ordinary rank-and-file member of the Labour Party and the average Labour voter were not very worried though more thoughtful members of local Labour Party management committees were. The Bevanite resignations probably harmed the Labour Party in the general election in October 1951. Without them Labour might just have scraped home again but no large section of the electorate had been alienated. The Labour Party has always been adept at presenting unbridgeable divisions among its members as healthy democratic discussion.

But now there was a dangerous new element in the disputes. One side, led by Nye Bevan and Harold Wilson, was relying on the support of Marxists and extremists whom normally they would have disdained. That is, they would have continued to disdain them if they had been able to fulfil their personal ambition for power by getting the moderate or orthodox element of the Parliamentary Labour Party to back them.

Frequently politicians have sought to make use of Communists and extremists to further their own advancement. They have usually ended up with a situation in which they themselves have been made use of to promote Communist and Marxist extremists. Once support is sought from, and association begun with, people who are not Social Democrats it is very difficult to avoid becoming uncomfortably enmeshed with them.

You cannot thank a man for his help one day, turn upon him the next and expect his help the following day. Mutual obligations and links emerge. The very act of relying upon the support of Marxists entails concessions to their viewpoints. That is the price they exact without ever deviating from their own rigid positions.

In turn, the larger grouping containing the extremists and the undercover Communists gets concessions from the Labour Party as a whole as the price for maintaining the façade of unity during an election campaign and in the eyes of the country between elections. The leaders of the dissident group adopt attitudes about further nationaliza-tion, and embrace illusions about the possibility of squeezing the rich to make everybody better off, which they do not really believe in but which they are forced to pretend they do to the Labour Party as a whole. Accordingly, as pressures grow, the leaders of the Labour Party feel obliged to put more and more nonsense into their Party programme in order to placate their internal enemies.

If Nye Bevan and Harold Wilson had been able to fulfil their ambitions entirely with the help of Social Democrats the Labour Party could have continued to be a reforming, but not overturning, Party as it was during Attlee's govern-ments. As they could not see a way to personal success through the Social Democrats alone they espoused causes which were unnatural to them. This was particularly true of Harold Wilson. More intelligent at political intrigues than Bevan he was more aware that he was supping with the Devil.

The tendency to trimming even affected a man of such integrity as Attlee. When Labour moved into Opposition he did little to defend, against the attacks of the extreme Left Wing, the rearmament programme which his Government had launched. He began to temper his pronouncements to the Left.

After he had done so on one occasion at a Parliamentary Labour Party meeting I was sitting in the Tea Room of the House of Commons with a like-minded Labour M.P. Both of us had been perturbed by Attlee's speech made in the more or less confidential circumstances of the Party meeting because it had been so different from what he had said when Prime Minister. Attlee knew what we were thinking. He came up to us and said, 'You can always say the same thing in Opposition as you did in Government, you know.' Doubtless that is true but Attlee had changed his approach not for electoral advantage, which might have been excusable, but to appease the Left Wing.

Some far-sighted members of the Labour Party understood what was going on. After the 1952 Labour conference Hugh Gaitskell made a speech at Stalybridge. In it he openly alleged that there had been distinct Communist infiltration among the delegates to the 1952 Labour Party conference at Morecambe. He went on to say, 'It is time to end the attempt at mob rule by a group of frustrated journalists and restore the authority and leadership of the solid, sound, sensible majority of the movement.' But the attempt was not ended nor was it being made solely by frustrated journalists.

In 1954 the issue of West German rearmament became important. The Bevanites were able to dispose of more strength than usual. Naturally the crypto-Communists, Marxists and extremists were on their side but this time the issue was so emotional that normally orthodox Labour M.P.s such as Dalton, the former Chancellor of the Exchequer, Chuter Ede, the former Home Secretary and James Callaghan, later to become Prime Minister, were corralled temporarily into the group.

It was smart and trendy within the Labour Movement, as well as a badge of sincere Socialism, to be against German rearmament. Indeed, my support for German rearmament meant that I had no seat with a Labour majority to stand for in the 1955 general election.

It came about this way. Since 1945 I had been the Member of Parliament for Aston in Birmingham. Alas, the Boundary Commissioners decided to redistribute the

Birmingham constituencies. Though the name Aston remained as the title of a constituency the three wards which had constituted it were added to three other separate constituencies which retained their original two wards apiece. One went to the new Aston constituency. Another went to Ladywood, whose M.P. was a pacifist and consequently against German rearmament. At the subsequent selection conferences my support for the official Party policy backing the Conservative Government's acceptance of German rearmament made it impossible for me to be selected. Julius Silverman became the M.P. for the newly structured Aston division. He was previously the member for Erdington, to which one ward of the old Aston division had been added. Silverman was ultra-Left Wing and against German rearmament.

The manner in which I came to have no seat between 1955 and 1959 illustrates the dangers in the Labour Party of not trimming to the populist clamour of the hour. It shows, too, the danger of supporting official Labour Party policy. If I had been in rebellion against it, I would have had no difficulty in getting selected for one of the Birmingham constituencies after redistribution of my own constituency. The fact that I was prepared to stand up for the leadership angered the extremists who were already beginning to have disproportionate influence in the management committees of local Labour Parties.

In the Parliamentary Labour Party itself, in February 1954, a resolution supporting the official policy on German rearmament got through by only 113 votes to 104. Though the Bevanites and the extremists had the support of a number of normally sensible people, who for emotional reasons could not stomach the idea of rearming Germany and who usually would not have sided with the Bevanites and extremists, nevertheless it represented a substantial advance for the Bevanites. It indicated that if they had the right issue or situation they could make considerable headway.

However, in those days the Labour Party National Executive remained stable. It approved the Parliamentary Labour Party's decision to support German rearmament —

something which in like circumstances it would not do today. The T.U.C. were also firm as they are not today. At their 1954 conference they supported German rearmament by 4,010,000 votes to 3,620,000. Likewise the Labour Party conference in the autumn supported it, albeit by the narrow margin of 3,270,000 to 3,020,000 votes. The narrowness of the victory was another illustration of how Bevanites and extremists were able to rally support when the going was good. But the victory for the Labour establishment also showed they were still in control in a way in which they are not now.

Incidentally, the opposition to German rearmament contrasts oddly with the current Left Wing complaint that Britain spends too high a percentage of her national income on defence compared with Germany and the other countries in the Western alliance. Without German rearmament the disproportion would be still greater and presumably few people seriously query now that Germany should make a physical contribution to her own defence, particularly as the East Germans are heavily armed. But logic never rated high among the extremists. As their sympathies are more with Russia and the Communist countries than with America, Britain and the democratic countries they are always prepared to use arguments dressed up as being in the interests of their own country while in practice being in the interests of the Communist-dominated countries.

I suppose if I had been in the starry-eyed condition I was in at the time of the *Keep Left* pamphlet seven years earlier I, too, might have opposed German rearmament. I certainly carried the usual prejudices prevailing so soon after the war against Germany and found it difficult to feel confidence in a nation responsible for two world wars – especially as I had been personally inconvenienced by having to spend over five and a half years in the Army during the second of them! But I had become enough of a realist to understand the need to stop extremists and crypto-Communists gaining strength by cloaking their real intentions in respectable association with Bevanites and Social Democrats who were not alert to what they were up to. Anyway it was long past the time when any intelligent person could believe that the new

Russian Communist empire was temporary or benevolent in intention either to its subjects or its neighbours.

Following upon the clash on German rearmament Nye Bevan, though a member of the Shadow Cabinet, attacked official policy which supported the Government's backing for the N.A.T.O. of the East — the South East Asia Treaty Organization. He resigned from the Shadow Cabinet and his place was eagerly taken by Harold Wilson who had been the unsuccessful runner-up for the elections for the Shadow Cabinet. Bevan continued with attacks on the Labour leadership and in February 1955 Bevan headed sixty-one rebels in the House of Commons in opposing official Labour policy on defence.

Whereupon a resolution was proposed and passed in the Parliamentary Party that in consequence of Bevan's persistent attacks on official Labour policy the Labour Party whip should be withdrawn from him. I did not vote for this motion though most of those who were my friends did. I believed that the expulsion of Nye Bevan could not be permanent, would drive him to greater association with extremists and enhance their strength.

I did not believe that Bevan was a genuine Bevanite but basically an acceptable Social Democrat unhinged by a passion for power which was not being satisfied. If he could feel that he had a secure place at the top of the Labour Party with a fair prospect of the eventual Leadership (though I did not want him to be Leader) his oratory and charisma would be on the side of Social Democracy and not of the extremists.

As it happened Attlee was evidently of the same opinion. He suggested in the Labour Party National Executive a compromise formula under which if Bevan promised to behave the Party whip would be restored to him. This was carried by a majority of one.

The effect was to gloss over to some extent the quarrels between the Labour Party leaders just before the general election of May 1955. And Nye Bevan, remaining in the fold, made it possible partially though not indefinitely to stem the advance of the extremists.

In December 1955 Attlee resigned. In the subsequent

Leadership contest Hugh Gaitskell won an overall majority against the other two candidates, Bevan and Herbert Morrison. Morrison got forty votes which it is reasonable to guess would have gone to Gaitskell had Morrison not stood. Add those to the 157 M.P.s who voted for Hugh Gaitskell and the score for common sense and orthodoxy was 197 to Bevan's seventy.

That seventy contained all the crypto-Communists, fellow-travellers, Marxists and extremists as well as the Social Democrats among the Bevanites. In figures the position was not much worse than it had been when R. H. S. Crossman got fifty-seven Labour M.P. rebels into the lobbies on the foreign affairs amendment to the Kings's Speech in November 1946.

Hugh Gaitskell was determined to make the Labour Party safe for Social Democracy. As he told me, he thought Attlee's style of leadership in Opposition too pusillanimous. Attlee tried too much to balance the disparate forces of the Party, he thought, and followed rather than led. Gaitskell set out to lead the Party without compromise with the Marxist and near-Communist elements. He was contemptuous of Wilson's method of pandering to the Left to get their support while reassuring the Right that he thought as they did.

This was the era of so-called Butskellism. The Tory Government were criticized for too high a level of unemployment (it was only 400,000 in 1959). They were attacked for setting up commercial television. They were accused of cheeseparing on social-security payments and failing to introduce a satisfactory system of superannuation pensions. The Tories were taunted for allowing Britain to drop behind other nations in raising productivity.

Among the targets were businessmen with tax-free expense accounts, speculators with tax-free capital gains, and tax-free handshakes for displaced company directors. The differences were more of emphasis than of principle.

Gaitskell thought and preached that the Tories had not gone far enough in egalitarianism but he did not propose to go so far as to wipe out differentials and incentives. To the demand within the Labour Party that there should be more

Socialism there was a reply which convinced most. Since the country had voted Tory in 1951 and 1955 because they wanted less Socialism what was the point of trying to get back into power by offering more?

But though that answer satisfied most it did not satisfy the extremists. Thwarted in the Parliamentary Labour Party they continued to make progress elsewhere. In 1956 the Communists and their allies very nearly captured control of the Amalgamated Engineering Union. They were only foiled by a television broadcast on the B.B.C. 'Panorama' programme urging members to vote in the current Presidential and Executive elections to prevent their union from moving out of the Social Democratic camp into the Communist orbit without their ever realizing what had happened.

That broadcast on 14 May 1956 increased the poll in the second ballot for the Presidency by more than forty per cent. W. J. Carron, whose failure to get an absolute majority in the first poll caused the second poll, thus defeated his Communist opponent by the largest majority for many years. There were similar results in the vote for seats on the National Executive of the Amalgamated Engineering Union. But the danger signals were flashing strongly.

In 1956, also, Frank Cousins became the General Secretary of the vast Transport and General Workers' Union. Immediately the T. & G.W.U. ceased to be one of the rocks on which the Labour leadership had always rested from the days of Ernest Bevin and Arthur Deakin. The General Secretary, with rare exceptions, rules the T. & G.W.U. single-handed because of the infrequency of meetings of the Executive. Despite the existence of an apparently democratic system it is he, and he alone, who in practice decides. As it was in the days of Arthur Deakin and Ernest Bevin so it became in the reign of Frank Cousins. He, with an ultra-Left Wing wife, was very much on the left. He supported the Bevanites and the extremists and was immensely hostile to the Labour leadership.

Frank Cousins' accession to control of the T. & G.W.U. was soon to have serious consequences. The mood of the Parliamentary Labour Party was equivocal with regard to trade-union affairs. Members without a trade-union background were supposed to mind their own business. I came under heavy fire for daring to intervene in the A.E.U. elections because, though I was not an M.P. at the time, it was known that I was trying to return. The trade-union M.P.s considered my action as unjustifiable interference and washing dirty linen in public. This despite the fact that they were Social Democrats themselves and could not possibly want the Communists to control the unions. Yet they preferred that they should do so rather than that they should be defeated from outside.

This attitude was still stronger over my television broadcasts on the Electricians' Union. The Communists were still in command and retaining their hold by cooking the union elections. It was thought very disloyal of me to point this out and to engage in a campaign to restore democracy to the Electricians' Union. I was expelled from the local Labour Party to which I belonged in London, which recommended that I should not be allowed to stand as a Labour candidate again. Fortunately Gaitskell, unhelped by Wilson, persuaded the National Executive to take no notice. Communists and extremists are considered all right because they are on the Left. Those who attack, expose and root them out are reprehensibly on the Right. Doing so ensured that I had no political future.

This explains why many moderate or orthodox Social Democrats dare not counter the Left strongly for fear of being undermined either in their local constituency parties or losing hope of office if they belong to the Parliamentary Labour Party. And those who hope for high office usually are careful to do little to offend union leaders; but more of that later.

So although the Parliamentary Labour Party looked healthy, the Party conference was beginning to turn against the leadership. Extremists were increasing their strength on the National Executive because of the changing leadership in the unions. That change in leadership approach was not desired by ordinary union members. It was imposed upon them by those who captured the important positions in the unions. For the zealots prepared to devote all their free hours to the task this is easier than might be supposed. The easy-going Social Democrat or orthodox Labour supporter is not besotted by politics and is not willing to give his life to acrimonious branch meetings and to slogging at the chores required of union officials all the way up and down the line.

Apparently, then, the Parliamentary Labour Party sat sane and sound to the public gaze and nominally in charge. Below, the woodworms were hollowing out the wood to make the structure unsafe. The Engineers' Union had not yet gone over to the other side but when it did so, maintaining Social Democracy in the Labour Party became immensely more difficult.

However, the defeat of Social Democracy was yet to come. In the meanwhile Labour went into the general election of 1959 with a cautious Social Democratic programme. The manifesto defended the nationalized industries and complained that the Tories had hobbled them. 'Under a Labour Government the nationalized industries will be given an opportunity once again to forge ahead.'

The only fresh nationalization promised was the renationalization of steel and commercial long-distance road haulage. 'We have no other plans for further nationalization.' There was a mild suggestion that 'Where an industry is shown, after thorough enquiry, to be failing the nation we reserve the right to take all or any part of it into public ownership if this is necessary. We shall also ensure that the community enjoys some of the profits and capital gains now going to private industry by arranging for the purchase of shares by public investment agencies such as the Superannuation Fund Trustees.'

This was the maximum concession to the Left Wing demand for more 'Socialism'. Gaitskell had won a general consent in the Party not to press unpopular nationalization as being the only means by which a Social Democratic Government could fulfil its aims to increase equal opportunity and egalitarianism.

The Labour Party was pointed for the time being in the same direction as that successfully pursued until the present by the Social Democratic parties of Scandinavia and West Germany.

CHAPTER SIX

Gaitskell fights and temporarily halts Encroachments of the Marxists and the ultra-Left

I F L A B O U R had won the October 1959 election all would have continued to look fair for Social Democracy. Gaitskell's authority would have been enhanced. He could have maintained an equable approach to economic policy and, with a distinguished economic background of his own, he could have guided both sides of industry into a secure cooperation with each other. Many of the industrial squabbles of the future would have been avoided and Britain would not have fallen so far behind her competitors. But Labour lost.

Gaitskell was certain that one of the main reasons was that the public did not believe that Labour had renounced nationalization. Despite the innocuous approach to nationalization in the recent election manifesto of the Labour Party clause four was still intact. Clause four was the only clause of the Labour Party's constitution printed on every membership card.

Labour's opponents had been able effectively to argue that Labour's apparent turning away from nationalization was both deceptive and temporary. Gaitskell determined on a frontal assault to rid Labour of the albatross. At a dinner at my house immediately after the election he was urged to do so by Roy Jenkins, Anthony Crosland and myself.

In 1959 the Labour Party conference at Blackpool was a shortened one because of the immediately preceding election. There Gaitskell put his case for removing from the Labour Party constitution the objects in clause four:

> To secure for the workers by hand or by brain the full fruits of their industry and the most equitable distribution thereof that may be possible, upon the basis of the common ownership of the means of production, distribution, and exchange, and the best obtainable system of popular administration and control of each industry or service.

It was a bad audience. The only supporter of the Labour establishment voted onto the National Executive by the constituency organizations' section at this conference was James Callaghan. And he, with an eye to the future, let the clamorous popular wind bend him rather than offend those to whom he looked for future advancement. Wedgwood Benn, too, had for the first time been voted onto the National Executive. Worse than that Frank Cousins, General Secretary of the Transport and General Workers' Union was now seeing himself as the new champion of the Left.

Gaitskell's was the classic Social Democratic position on public ownership. Attacking clause four and its status as the main declaration of faith printed on the membership card he said:

> It lays us open to continual misrepresentation. It implies that common ownership is an end, whereas in fact it is a means. It implies that the only object we have is nationalization, whereas we have in fact many other Socialist objectives. It implies that we propose to nationalize everything. But do we? Everything? The whole of light industry, the whole of agriculture, of the shops, every little pub and garage? [At this point there were many shouts of 'Yes'.] Of course not. We have long ago come to accept, we know very well for the foreseeable future at least in some form, a mixed economy. In which case, if this is our view, as I believe it to be of ninety per cent of the Labour Party, had we better not say so instead of going out of our way to court misrepresentation?

But ninety per cent of the Labour Party were not represented in the hall. It was the voice of the ten per cent which was there. It was there to a greater extent than ever before.

Immediately Gaitskell was attacked by Frank Cousins. 'We have all accepted in the past that, while we can have nationalization without Socialism, we cannot have Socialism without nationalization. Those who make any other form of approach are doing a disservice to the Labour Movement.'

Nye Bevan, winding up the debate and now Deputy Leader of the Party, did not exactly attack his Leader. Bevan's position was strong. He was Treasurer of the Party, elected by the combined votes of the trade-union and constituency sections of the Party conference. Gaitskell had made him spokesman for foreign affairs and there had been something of a reconciliation. So much so that in the 1957 Party conference Bevan had emerged openly on the side of Social Democracy. In a reply to a motion demanding the unilateral renunciation by Britain of all atomic weapons he had cogently argued that such a renunciation would send a British Foreign Secretary naked into the conference chamber. The love of the Left Wing activists for him was sufficient for the resolution to be defeated. But though Bevan did not openly attack Gaitskell in the clause four conference debate he skirted the issue by insisting that public ownership should be kept in the Labour programme.

Gaitskell did not give up immediately. He persuaded the National Executive to frame another interpretation to clause four. It would have been an improvement. In part it read, 'Recognizing that both public and private enterprise have a place in the economy it believes that further extensions of common ownership should be decided from time to time in the light of these objectives according to circumstances, with due regard for the views of the workers and consumers concerned.'

Elsewhere in the re-interpretation was included the proposition that the Labour Party's 'social and economic objectives can be achieved only through the extension of common ownership substantial enough to give the community power over commanding heights of the economy.'

The fatuous and meaningless words, 'commanding heights of the economy', were of course taken from a phrase once used by Nye Bevan. But even this attempted compromise with the extremists did not satisfy them. Cousins denounced Gaitskell's views as being contrary to Socialism. A group of extremists with some strength in the Party and called 'Victory for Socialism' demanded Gaitskell's resignation. On 13 July 1960 the National Executive announced that it would not proceed with any amendment or addition to clause four of the constitution. So, to the delight of the extremists and Marxists, the Labour Party's membership card still flaunts it.

It may be that the onward march of the extremists could have been halted there if Bevan had not died in July 1960. He had accepted that so long as Gaitskell lived he would be supported by the Parliamentary Labour Party and that any aspirations beyond the second place were unrealistic. But in the unpredictable way of politics Gaitskell might die or disappear and Bevan, if his behaviour were tolerable, would get the reversion. And his second place was a powerful one. There was every prospect that the two leaders would remain for some time. In 1960 Bevan was a mere sixty-two and Gaitskell fifty-four. No great ages in politics and, with the growth of interdependence between the two, Social Democracy was becoming more secure, particularly as, however vivid his language, Nye Bevan was moderate in what he wanted to do.

Gaitskell's defeat over clause four gave fresh zest to the Marxists, crypto-Communists, fellow-travellers and extremists. Fervent advocates of more and more State control through increased bouts of nationalization, they were encouraged. They could correctly foresee a future in which every Labour manifesto would have to promise at each election some fresh nationalization to satisfy the zealots. Provided that a year or two followed each act of nationalization before the Tories returned to office each new piece of nationalization would become irreversible. It is very difficult to sell back to private enterprise something which has been ruined by nationalization and which a new Labour Government will renationalize with even less compensation or possibly with none at all.

Cumulatively the process gradually puts a growing

percentage of industry into the hands of the State with the appalling consequences examined later. Productivity was never of any interest to the extremists. They would rather control men's lives in uniform misery according to their definition of the public good than allow them to flourish freely.

In 1960 the most promising cause for overthrowing the Labour leadership was that of unilateral nuclear disamament. Many well-meaning but intellectually backward people, especially among the young, had been persuaded that their nuclear destruction was imminent. Futile protest marches from the atomic research centre at Aldermaston to Trafalgar Square were undertaken and were very popular at Easter. Those like Michael Foot, Barbara Castle, Tony Greenwood and Frank Cousins, anxious to curry favour with those who considered themselves true Socialists, ostentatiously joined in the demonstrating. That they could not have been very sincere was evidenced by their happily taking office subsequently in Labour Governments more heavily armed with the power of nuclear destruction than any that went before them.

Not that they were alone in their hypocrisy. Others of their comrades flaunted themselves at unilateral nuclear disarmament meetings and later satisfied themselves that their consciences were in order when they received and accepted the call to office. Judith Hart, Peter Shore and others all thought their passionate support for unilateral nuclear disarmament was of secondary importance to ministerial position.

The campaign for unilateral nuclear disarmament seems utterly ridiculous now. I don't know what has happened to it. But if it had any validity in the 1950s and 60s it should have as much validity today. The world has not got fewer nuclear weapons but far more. Britain is still capable by herself of wiping out the major Russian cities with nuclear weapons. But it was not the purpose of many at the head of the campaign seriously to achieve unilateral nuclear disarmament.

Their purpose was to garner together a disparate force of cranks and Communists, of the well-meaning naive who did not know the object for which they were being used, of extremists, of Marxists, of Social Democrats a little soft in the head. It was all deliciously trendy and got mixed up with equality for women and what the younger generation were supposed to think (what do they think now they are older?). It was a way of whipping up enthusiasm for extremist candidates seeking positions in the trade unions. It was a splendid weapon against the Labour leadership.

If the Labour leadership could be vanquished or forced out over the issue the greater the dent in Social Democracy. Not that all who supported the campaign realized that this was the aim of the chief organizers. But it was. And the campaign did lasting damage to the democratic outlook of the Labour Party. It stimulated the growth of the idea that Britain and America in hanging on to nuclear weapons for self-defence were taking an unreasonably aggressive attitude towards Russia. Dominant in the campaign were those who sympathized with the Soviet Union and the Communist Parties tyrannizing Eastern Europe. The Russian Communists were never criticized for their huge nuclear armouries but were ludicrously sympathized with for being forced by the wicked West to have them.

It is incredible that people who wished to be taken seriously should contemplate a unilateral disarmament leaving the West totally defenceless in the face of the Kremlin. It is incredible that a number of them should have eventually been given office in a British Government. But it was so. All during the summer of 1960 the infection, assiduously spread by those among the leadership of the campaign who knew what they were about, claimed increasing numbers of victims among the constituency Labour Parties and among union officials.

No one on the Left of the Labour Party dared to be immune from the disease. By October 1960 when the Labour Party conference was held at Scarborough the position was grim. The National Committee of the A.E.U. had been undermined by Communists and their sympathizers. The A.E.U. delegation was instructed to cast its mammoth block vote against the official defence policy. Gleefully, Frank Cousins moved a resolution on behalf of

66

the T. & G.W.U. calling for 'A complete rejection of any defence policy based on the threat of the use of strategic or tactical nuclear weapons'.

It was Frank Cousins' revenge for Gaitskell's attempt to scratch out clause four. It was also his demonstration that he intended the Labour Party to go the way that he and his ultra-Left Wing wife wanted it to go rather than the way preferred by the vast majority of Labour voters and the Parliamentary Labour Party.

Disloyalty to the official position was deep at Labour Party headquarters. Officials such as Peter Shore flaunted their C.N.D. badges to indicate to everyone that they did not support the views of the organization to which they owed their allegiance. With the major unions casting their block votes against the official policy, not because their members wanted them to but because their leaders had decided that it was politically fruitful, the platform had no chance.

Nevertheless Gaitskell fought back. He knew that if the Labour Party entered the next election pledged to neutralism and unilateral nuclear disarmament they would have no hope of winning. Refusal to abandon adherence to ever more nationalization added to an open invitation to the Russians to take us over would promote to a certainty the apprehension in the public mind that the Labour Party was going towards some form of Communism.

Gaitskell declared, 'There are some of us who will fight and fight and fight again to save the Party we love. We will fight and fight and fight again to bring back sanity and honesty and dignity so that our Party with its great past may retain its glory and its greatness.'

While his colleagues on the platform applauded Gaitskell's fighting speech, Wilson, the arch-trimmer of British politics, remained conspicuously impassive and silent. The message was plain. He was committed as a member of the Shadow Cabinet to everything that Gaitskell said, and he had not opposed it within that Shadow Cabinet, but he wanted to pretend to those with whom the tide was flowing that at heart he was with them. If he had been truly with them he would have pursued the abandonment of the nuclear deterrent when he became Prime Minister in 1964. Instead he maintained our own independent nuclear deterrent and added to it the Polaris submarines which we had bought from America – while feebly explaining that since they were American in origin they could not truly be called an independent British deterrent.

The day before the Gaitskell defeat there had been an attempt completely to subordinate the Parliamentary Labour Party to the Party conference. To dodge that, the National Executive accepted a diluted resolution which left the question of the mastership of the Parliamentary Labour Party open. Among other things this resolution declared that the policy of the Labour Party in Parliament on questions of principle should be determined by annual conferences. It acknowledged that the Parliamentary Labour Party had to deal with day-to-day tactics but 'This conference declares that Labour policy is decided by the Party conference, which is the final authority.'

So the campaign for unilateral nuclear disarmament had done a lot for those with the most drive in it and whose aim was to turn the Labour Party away from Social Democracy. For the moment the Party conference was in their hands.

For the first time I felt that it might not be possible to keep the Labour Party on a democratic course. Not long after I told Hugh Gaitskell that I thought he might not be Leader of the Labour Party in a year's time.

Many high in the Labour Party were fearful of Gaitskell's determination to reverse the decision of the Party conference and tried to dissuade him from it. They thought that in the ensuing civil war the Labour Party might be smashed. Ever ready to draw back from a fight for principle, Harold Wilson offered himself as a candidate to the Party Leadership when Parliament reassembled after the October Labour conference. True, he was reluctant but he was told by his supporters and Anthony Greenwood that if he did not carry the banner for appeasement to the nuclear disarmers and their extremist henchmen then Anthony Greenwood would.

With the double stance of believing in the Parliamentary

Labour Party's attitude towards nuclear disarmament, while ensuring that it would not be implemented, Harold Wilson stood against Gaitskell. He was defeated by 166 votes to eighty-one. Though that was a majority of over two to one it was alarming that there were eighty-one Labour M.P.s now firmly against Gaitskell's ideal of keeping the Labour Party a Social Democratic one.

What happened afterwards was another illustration of the bogus nature of the union block vote cast at Labour Party conferences. No rank-and-file members changed their views between the two conferences of 1960 and 1961. Or if they did there could not have been more than a handful. Yet persistent lobbying among trade-union leaders by Gaitskell and his friends persuaded them to work to change their union votes.

Notable among the campaigners was W. T. Rodgers, later to become Minister of Transport in a Labour Government. Largely due to his energy a group called the Campaign for Democratic Socialism was organized and went to work in the constituencies and among trade-union officials. The official Labour policy was now fuzzed at the edges by a suggestion that Britain should give up the attempt to be an independent nuclear power (which we never did) but it maintained that the West should not renounce nuclear weapons so long as the Russians had them.

The Union of Shop, Distributive and Allied Workers, the Amalgamated Engineering Union and the National Union of Railwaymen announced that they were changing sides. The Electrical Trades Union by this time had been disaffiliated from the Labour Party because its leaders' fraudulent practices in cooking the votes had at last been officially recognized. Thus their vote in favour of unilateral nuclear disarmament could not be delivered at the Party conference in 1961.

Miraculously the defeat of 1960 was turned into the victory of 1961. The official defence policy denouncing unilateral nuclear disarmament was carried by 4,526,000 votes against 1,756,000. A substantial part of the contrary votes were delivered by Frank Cousins who refused to change his position though obviously his members did not in the slightest agree with him. But Frank Cousins, despite his protestations of democracy, had no belief in it – though he was greatly annoyed when I described him in a speech as 'the bully with the block vote'. But the new conditions for attack from the Left were in the shaping. Foiled in their efforts to use the dispute on clause four and the argument about nuclear weapons to displace Gaitskell, the pro-Communists, Marxists, extremists and their allies in the Labour Party were beginning to find a new issue wherewith the innocent and not so innocent could be directed towards capturing the Labour Party. It was the growing prospect that Britain one day might join the Common Market.

No one of significance on the Left Wing of the Labour Party, save for a short time Eric Heffer, ever supported Britain's entry into the Common Market. It was true that genuine Social Democrats like Douglas Jay were always against it but it was never the other way round. Why not? Because the Kremlin strongly disliked anything which could lead to a more united Western Europe. The weaker Western Europe is the better the chance of extending Soviet influence whether physically from outside or by encouraging the growth of Communist Parties internally. The anti-Common Market campaign was to become a plentiful hunting-ground for the extremists. There were even Conservatives on their side making their activities appear extraordinarily respectable.

The jingoism of Little England could be harnessed to darker purposes. There were many like Eden, Attlee and Douglas Jay who instinctively felt that it was dangerous to consort with foreigners. In Attlee's case the territory occupied by undesirable aliens began at Calais and only ceased on arrival at Bombay though he combined this distrust of foreigners with a curiously premature association with a campaign for world government.

Not long after the war I attended at Königswinter a conference run by an Anglo-German friendship society. Among the participants was Douglas Jay, venturing abroad. For our meals we sat on benches in front of long wooden tables. One morning at breakfast I found myself sitting opposite Douglas Jay. He had a number of large brown envelopes scattered around his place. Out of one of them he took Shredded Wheat, out of another Grapenuts, out of another cornflakes and so on. Seeing my interest he said, 'Can't trust these foreigners with breakfast. Always take mine with me when I go abroad. They might give you cheese or something like that.' It was not a complete surprise to me when some years afterwards he announced his vehement opposition to Britain joining the Common Market.

I never knew quite what Hugh Gaitskell really thought about Britain and the Common Market. Through a family tradition of service in India he had a strong devotion to the new Commonwealth which the old British Empire turned into. Immigration to him was a matter of *civis Romanus sum*. All coloured immigrants had once belonged to the Empire. Now they belonged to the new Commonwealth and Britain was still their mother, though not their imperial, country. Anyone who had been a citizen of the British Empire or was a citizen of the new Commonwealth, for him had the absolute right to travel and settle in any part of it, including metropolitan Britain.

I do not know how long Gaitskell would have maintained his backing for unlimited immigration. By the time he died it was an important problem in Britain but not over-whelmingly so. Would he have called a halt at one and a half million immigrants, two million, three million, five or ten million? I do not know. The original principles with which he started out on the subject logically would not have allowed him to ask for an end to immigration at any level though circumstances must surely have forced him to change his mind. Presumably he would have come to agree with the restrictions which were eventually put on immigration.

As the uselessness of the new Commonwealth emerged his realism would have compelled him to acknowledge that it was not much of a success as a coherent community of nations. He could not have continued to convince himself that the alternative to being in an effective grouping like the Common Market was to remain the centre of a non-functioning Commonwealth. But at that time he still had his honourable hopes and delusions. Apart from the new members of the Commonwealth, Australia, New Zealand and Canada were then much more committed to us than they are today.

There was also a weariness in him. He had fought a great battle for clause four and lost. He had fought once against unilateral nuclear disarmament and been defeated. He had fought again with all his energy to reverse this defeat and had succeeded. Psychologically I do not think he was able to take on another fight against the screaming Left Wing over the Common Market.

His main political friends and allies were pro-Common Market. They would have liked him to be the same. Obviously he felt the pull from them. But the pull was not strong enough to overcome his unthinking, as distinct from his thinking, objections.

Nor did he yet see how potent an instrument the Common Market issue would be in the hands of those who hated every Social Democratic value which he wished to see embedded in the Labour Party. After much campaigning and many speeches all over the country, bolstered in his tiredness by pills, the various factors combined to put him against Britain joining the Common Market. At least, against it unless a number of conditions, several of which were impossible, were met. It must have been with relief that he felt he could for once speak without being subjected to the malevolent, vicious, vituperative attacks of the pro-Communists, Marxists and their general ragbag of sympathizers. Thus he made a remarkable speech at his last Labour Party conference in October 1962. For Britain to enter the Common Market, he rousingly declaimed, would be the end of a thousand years of history.

Unusually, he had a raptuous reception at a Labour Party conference. But unwittingly he had made it harder for his friends to hold the Social Democratic line from the beginning of the next decade. If he had been alive the changing situation would surely have caused him to modify the conditions he laid down and to understand why Britain could only hope for a renewed or continuing influence in the world through the European Community and not through

72

the new Commonwealth. He would have come to appreciate that Western Europe needed Britain as well as Britain, to survive adequately, needed to join a larger group.

Though I realized it but dimly at the time, Hugh Gaitskell's sad death on 11 January 1963 was a blow to the steady hope of keeping the Social Democratic ethos uppermost in the Labour Party so great that it was almost mortal. As he had said he would, Gaitskell had led the Labour Party from in front and not from behind. Though he had not wrenched clause four out of the Constitution the electorate understood that it would have no meaning so long as he was Leader. With the exception of Frank Cousins of the T. & G.W.U., Gaitskell had re-established the close sympathy between the Parliamentary leadership and the trade-union leadership which had existed in Attlee's time.

Undoubtedly Gaitskell's leadership was the reason why the Labour Party won the election in 1964, the year after his death. He had, as he had promised, returned it to sanity. For the time being it looked settled and sound, just as it had done between 1945 and 1951.

If Gaitskell had lived Labour would have won a majority larger than the four with which it scraped home. There would have been no need for an election in 1966. Fifty-six when he died he might reasonably have been expected to have lived and to have been Leader until he was at least sixty-five. That would have given him eight years to consolidate the Labour Party on Social Democratic lines and to make it proof against the depredations of the Communists, crypto-Communists and all the rest gathered on the ultra-Left Wing. For a time the momentum of what he had done carried the Labour Party forward successfully. Harold Wilson was the beneficiary of his achievement; but he squandered it.

CHAPTER SEVEN

After Gaitskell's Death, the Slide to the ultra-Left quickens

THE DEATH of Hugh Gaitskell put the Social Democrat majority in the Parliamentary Labour Party not only into consternation but into a horrid dilemma. In 1961 Alfred Robens had accepted the chairmanship of the National Coal Board. It was an understandable decision. Active and able, a doer rather than a talker, he had had ten frustrating years talking in the House of Commons since Labour's defeat in 1951. Those years were a big chunk of his prime. In Attlee's Government he had held office for four years, finishing as Minister of Labour in the Cabinet.

Ten years must have seemed a very long time to have waited for some useful occupation to turn up again. Gaitskell, after Bevan's death, had made him spokesman for foreign affairs. He was not very good at it and the role showed how unsuitable life on the Opposition benches is for a man who wishes to be creative and to use his talents when those talents are less fitted to debating issues than to taking practical measures about them.

When Robens went to the National Coal Board, where he was an outstanding success, he could not have contemplated that within two years Gaitskell would be dead. With Gaitskell as Prime Minister there was always the prospect of a return to active politics in an important Ministry. If he had foreseen Gaitskell's death Robens obviously would have stayed in the Parliamentary Labour Party since he would have been almost certain to succeed him. He was tough but sensible. He had the qualities of a leader. The Social Democrats would have backed him enthusiastically. But with Robens gone the solid man of the Right with most chance of success was George Brown.

George Brown was frequently violent and erratic. Often he lacked dignity and drank too much. Unquestionably he was a sound Social Democrat but his temperament alarmed, not without reason, many of the Social Democrats.

The third candidate in the contest was James Callaghan. He was felt by many Labour M.P.s to be too willing to subordinate what he thought to be right to the interests of his personal political career. But to some Social Democrats he seemed a better bet than either Wilson or Brown. Yet to others Wilson's trickiness was more than outweighed by the mercurial nature of George Brown's character and the inferior brainpower of the too ambitious James Callaghan. After all, Wilson had been barely a Bevanite and was at heart a Right Winger, however much he found it expedient to convey the opposite.

Like eighty-seven others, with some misgivings, I voted for George Brown but I would gladly have voted for Robens had he been there. The Social Democrats were hopelessly divided. Forty-one voted for Callaghan and some forty to fifty must have voted for Wilson which, added to the ragbag of extreme Left Wingers, gave him a score of 115 on the first ballot. Wilson thus became Leader and the acceleration of the decline in Social Democracy in the Labour Party began.

Without the support of the Communists, crypto-Communists and their associates and friends on the very Left Wing, Wilson could not have been elected. They were the base of his victory and he was always conscious of it. For the rest of his career he was unable or unwilling to shake them off.

So entered the period of Labour leadership in which, to keep the unity of the Party, a balance was always struck between Right and Left. This was quite contrary to Gaitskell's method of leadership. He decided on the correct course and those who would be most likely to help him succeed in carrying it through. He did not balance a common-sense Social Democratic move with another simultaneously designed to please the Left. If he had been Prime Minister he would not have put into significant positions in his Government very Left Wing figures by way

75

of apologizing for including sensible Social Democrats.

The Labour Party manifesto for the October 1964 election was moderate enough. But when Wilson had won he made a typical gesture of appeasement to the Left. Not only did he include R. H. S. Crossman and Barbara Castle in his Cabinet, he invited Frank Cousins to join it as Minister of Technology. Frank Cousins was a man of no ability whatever. He was there to convince the extreme Left that Wilson was still on their side. Outside the Cabinet he made numerous ultra-Left Wingers junior Ministers for the same reasons. Thus did the style of the Labour leadership change immediately.

With its tiny majority of four the Labour Government of 1964 was in no position to do anything very dramatic. However, they chose to press on with the nationalization of steel. This had been, apart from the promise to bring water undertakings under full public ownership (which has never been accomplished), the only proposal for new nationalization. It was in effect a determination to complete the nationalization of steel begun by the Attlee Government but halted by the Tories in 1951.

After thirteen years conditions had changed. There was considerable experience of the workings of the nationalized industries. Industrial relations were no better in them, save in the coal-mines, than they had been when they were privately owned. In some cases they were worse. Productivity in the nationalized industries was way below that in the private sector. They had received a much higher proportion of national resources than the private sector without making a corresponding contribution to increased wealth.

There was nothing freshly democratic about their organization. There was as little participation by the workers in how their places of work should be run as there had been before. Any stimulus which might have been provided previously by the profit motive had been stifled by the bureaucratic interference of Whitehall. Without the profit motive waste and extravagance had accumulated.

The determination to renationalize steel was born not of expectation that the nation would benefit but out of doctrinaire zealotry. It was a blind worship of clause four which Hugh Gaitskell had tried to eradicate.

This seemed to me an issue on which Social Democrats should stick. The mix between public and free enterprise was about right: maybe public ownership had already gone too far. But it was too late to unscramble what had been done even in the few instances where it might have been practicable. The original notion that steel would give great planning powers to Governments enabling them to dictate the shape and purpose of the rest of British industry was now antiquated. It was not one of Nye Bevan's 'commanding heights of the economy' any more. It was just one among several important industries.

The Government had ample control over its activities through the Iron and Steel Board set up by the Conservatives. The old-fashioned blanket nationalization of steel could not be justified unless it could be demonstrated with some certainty that nationalization would increase its competitiveness and efficiency.

As it is, the public ownership of steel has well nigh wrecked it. In 1975 metric tonnes of steel produced per head per year in the British steel industry compared as follows: Japan 372, U.S.A. 274, Netherlands 243, Italy 232, Germany 225, France 164, Britain 131.

In 1967, the year steel was nationalized, we imported 2,194,000 metric tonnes of iron and steel and exported 4,159,000 metric tonnes. After eight years of nationalization in 1975 we had to import 4,206,000 tonnes of iron and steel and our exports had sunk to 3,391,000 tonnes of steel thus creating an adverse balance which never occurred before nationalization.

Attempts at modernization and reduced manning have been frustrated, delayed or thwarted by the unions. Frequent governmental changes of plans and intentions have made orderly management impossible. British Steel now performs worse than the steel industry of any other industrial country. It is a shameful monument to Socialist evangelism. Whether it remains nationalized or not there must be considerable doubt that it can now raise itself to the standards of our competitor countries.

In the first flash of enthusiasm for public ownership I did not foresee this danger in the 1945–51 Parliament. But by 1964 I had seen enough of what went on in industry to know the disaster total nationalization of steel would be. In their hearts I am sure that many Social Democrats in the Labour Party thought the same.

The difficulty was that the nationalization of steel had been included in the Labour manifesto because to leave it out would have provoked an almighty row. It was, as it were, the statutory showpiece of nationalization which must be written into every Labour manifesto to placate the extremists. If Gaitskell had won over clause four it might have been a different matter; but he had not won.

Senior politicians in the Labour Party were quite cynical about it. They knew that steel nationalization could do nothing but harm to the country but feared that it would ruin their personal political careers if they said so and if it were not carried through. They sought to minimize the damage which would be done and even unconvincingly attempted to argue that nationalization would be an improvement. As an alternative to that they argued that whether steel were nationalized or not would make little difference to the economy, and, as it would keep the Left Wing quiet for a bit, why not let it go through?

Accepting that there might be a case, if not a very strong one, for some increased public control I proposed a compromise. It was simply that the State should own fifty-one per cent of the shares in the steel enterprises and that the general public should own the remaining forty-nine per cent. Steel would then be run as a normal commercial concern and not by civil servants who are utterly incompetent to run businesses. The Government's fifty-one per cent would enable it to remove any Chairman or members of the Board they thought were inefficient or acting contrary to public policy. That fifty-one per cent would also give the Government power to influence major policy decisions though not the day-to-day decisions as to whether there should be rationalization of steelworks, closures, introduction of new processes and so on. The Government rein would be loose as it is with British

Petroleum, one of our most successful companies, in which the Government have a dominating shareholding.

The rein would have to be loose because the general public, particularly through the financial institutions which would presumably have had large holdings of shares, would insist on economy and profitability. With so large a private shareholding steel could not be run, as in large part it has been run, as a branch of social security maintaining jobs which should be ended. Having no need to account to shareholders and able to rely on Government subsidies, British Steel has not been under the driving pressure it should have been to end overmanning and to become profitable. It has also had the disadvantage of Government interference in the fixing of its prices which is a matter which should have been left to commercial judgment.

During the election campaign of October 1964 I had been careful to say that while I accepted the manifesto in broad terms I did not accept the old-fashioned nationalization of steel. I said then that I thought that such nationalization would be arid and unconstructive. What was needed with the management and controllers of industry was not confrontation and orders from Whitehall but cooperation. The marriage should be between the resources of the State and the energies and enthusiasm of free enterprise. So I was not breaking faith with the electors or with the Labour Party when I took my stand against the nationalization of steel in the 1964 Parliament.

I hoped that my preventing the nationalization of steel, with the aid of Desmond Donnelly (who in fact wanted no change whatever), would give the Labour Party a chance to reconsider its position and find a more germinal solution. Since Labour's majority by this time was down to three the Cabinet lost its nerve and did not proceed with nationalization in that Parliament. Thus the Labour Party did get a chance to think again but it decided not to take it though many in the Labour Party thought it would have been wise to do so.

Why did not other Social Democrats who thought as I did speak out? Why did not those experienced leaders of the Labour Party who knew what damage the nationalization of steel would do to the country try to alter the manner of it? Because courage among Social Democrats in the Labour Party is too scarce. Frequently they know what is right but they dare not say it. They are afraid of being undermined in their constituencies – a very real fear. They are afraid of losing votes in contests for the Shadow Cabinet if their Socialist faith is queried. They dislike the rumpus that opposition to the Left Wing of the Labour Party entails. So they tend to be quiet and peaceable. They do not want to take any stand that they can avoid which might lead to the accusation that they are splitting the Party.

It is this weakness in the moral fibre of the Social Democrats which is one of the main dangers to Social Democracy. The Social Democrats would have been far tougher if Gaitskell had lived or Robens had been Prime Minister. For example, either might well have accepted the fifty-one per cent compromise on steel and persuaded the free enterprise owners of the steel firms to accept it too. A departure of this kind from old-fashioned blanket nationalization would have broken the grip that the obsession with more and more nationalization has upon the Labour Party. It would have encouraged Social Democrats to speak bravely and rationally and not always to conform to conventional Labour Party rigidity. It would have been an opportunity to change the entire direction of the un-satisfactory methods by which public ownership is controlled.

But Wilson was not the man to initiate any radical changes in the Labour Party approach. His method was to maintain himself at the head of the Labour Party by deft concessions to any block which might threaten him if not placated. He could count on the loyalty of the Social Democrats but not on that of the extreme Left Wing to whom he owed so much. He never ventured to annoy the latter unless he thought that his position in the country, and hence his future in the Premiership, would be damaged by leaning too much in their direction when the popular mood was overwhelmingly the other way. His was a balancing act. He did not believe that the country as a whole cared whether

80

steel were nationalized or not but he did believe that there were other things they felt strongly about.

Accordingly Wilson by the time of the general election of March 1966 was still holding more or less to Social Democratic tenets. He profited electorally from the gains made by Hugh Gaitskell and did not immediately dissipate them. When he won the general election in March 1966 his majority went up from three to ninety-seven. This gave him added confidence in two directions. One, with an enhanced personal prestige and larger majority he felt safe in implementing old-fashioned steel nationalization despite its unpopularity in the country. Two, he also felt sure enough of himself to defy the extreme Left Wing a little in the national interest.

In May 1966 the seamen went on strike. Britain, as usual, was suffering from chronic economic deficiencies and a severe balance-of-payments problem. The strike, and the damage it caused to our exports, greatly worsened our economy. It lasted forty-seven days.

During the course of it Wilson, enraged by the National Union of Seamen, made an attack on its Executive Council quite out of keeping with his normal behaviour. In Parliament he said,

> It has been apparent for some time —— and I do not say this without having a good reason for saying it ——that since the Court of Inquiry's report a few individuals have brought pressure to bear on a select few of the Executive Council of the National Union of Seamen who in turn have been able to dominate the majority of that otherwise sturdy union. It is difficult for us to appreciate the pressures which are being put on men I know to be realistic and responsible, not only in their executive capacity but in the highly organized strike committees in the ports, by this tightly knit group of politically motivated men . . .

Wilson meant that there were Communists manipulating the union for their own political ends and not in the interests of their members or the country. Characteristically he did not say so openly.

Listening to his statement I could not help laughing. Here was a man, who had given me no support in the battle against the crooked Communist dictators of the E.T.U. or in the battle to prevent the Communists and their fellow-travellers dominating the Engineers' Union, saying what I had been saying for years. When his own position was threatened he was quick enough to preach the virtues of Social Democracy but could not be persuaded to risk the anger of the extreme Left in stating the obvious truth until he was personally involved. This kind of cowardice, interspersed by brief spurts of bravery, coloured his whole leadership and was a principal cause of the decline in the hold which Social Democracy had in the Labour Party.

Because of the harm done by the seamen's strike it was necessary in the summer to introduce a prices and wages standstill or freeze. Some Labour M.P.s, mostly the extreme Left, were inevitably against the necessary measures. A by-product of the prices and wages freeze was the resignation of Frank Cousins. He had been a failure as a Minister and was doubtless happy to use his opposition to the standstill on wages as a reason for returning to his job as General Secretary of the Transport and General Workers' Union. The Left Wing thus got back again a strident champion who was extremely useful to the anti-Social Democrats among them.

In September 1966 at the T.U.C. Conference Cousins was behind the motion against wages legislation which was defeated by a mere 474,000 out of a total of nearly nine million. Real trouble was ahead.

In 1967 there was another setback to Social Democracy. The very Left Wing Hugh Scanlon was elected President of the Engineers' Union. There was considerable doubt about the validity of the result. There had been questionable activities in the union branches in the Manchester area. As I had played a considerable part previously in exposing union malpractices I was approached to do something about this election.

To my everlasting shame I did little or nothing. I did not feel inclined once more to incur the hostility of the trade-union M.P.s, most of whom were solid Social Democrats, who could not bear the idea of outside interference in union matters. I was suffering from the malaise which overcomes Social Democrats after long attacks upon them for trying to uphold democratic methods against totalitarianism. So Scanlon's election went without successful challenge. By this time the Executive of the Engineers' Union had also slipped and could usually be counted upon to support the new President in his anti-Social Democratic approach.

There were now two union block votes large enough usually to swing the vote any way they liked at Labour Party and T.U.C. conferences. There was no change in this when Frank Cousins was succeeded by the even more Left Wing Jack Jones in 1969. Jones did not even have the slight restraint on his irrationality which Ministerial responsibility just conceivably gave to Frank Cousins.

The union leaders were beginning to sense their power and to use it irrespective of their members' wishes. The new alliance between the orthodox Labour leadership and the trade-union leaders made afresh by Hugh Gaitskell was now too broken to give effective support to a Labour Cabinet. Frank Cousins, Jack Jones, Hugh Scanlon were the allies of the dissident Bevanites, Tribunites, Marxists and the ultra-Left Wing assortment in the Parliamentary Labour Party. Previously the Labour Cabinets could be brave enough to stand up often to the extremists in the Parliamentary Labour Party knowing that those extremists were isolated in the wider Labour Movement, because they lacked trade-union support. Now the cabinet were no longer in that position and they lacked the necessary toughness of mind.

Because of Harold Wilson's appeasement policy of including Left Wingers in his Government, the Labour Government and Cabinet were themselves undermined by an extremist fifth column. In 1968 it was still not understood that the making of Labour's policies was irreversibly moving into quite different hands. The days in which an Attlee Government made up its mind and was loyally and unquestioningly supported by union leaders who could not be defeated at the Labour Conference had now passed for ever. The events of 1969 illustrated this dramatically.

83

The Donovan Royal Commission on the trade unions had sat from 1965 to 1968. The condition of the unions was appalling. Ernest Bevin as Britain's Labour Foreign Secretary had been able to create for West Germany a modern trade-union structure. It was based on the principle of one union for each major industry. Instead of having over four hundred, as in Britain, the West Germans had, counting those both inside and outside industry, only twenty. Inter-union disputes could not arise. The union leaders were emphatically Social Democratic, uninfluenced by Marxism. They and their members were united in extolling the profit motive and in furthering the interests of the concerns for which they worked. Hence West Germany's rising prosperity.

It was obvious that Britain's unions were inappropriate for modern industrial society. The multiplicity of unions meant, and still does mean, incessant squabbling over demarcation and which union has the right to do what. Overmanning, and resistance to new equipment which might reduce that overmanning, prevailed and still does. Strikes, official and unofficial, disfigured the industrial landscape and still do. Union leaders did not represent their members because they were elected on defective procedures or because once elected, as in the Transport and General Workers' Union, they were there for life. They are still largely unrepresentative without much hope of change.

The feeling in the country was that something should and could be done to reform the unions. It was a prerequisite to industrial progress. The view was confirmed by the Donovan Commission. The next general election could not be delayed beyond the beginning of 1971. Reforming the unions would win votes so Wilson was attracted by the proposition though he knew the Left would not like it.

In January 1969 Barbara Castle, Secretary for Employment, produced her White Paper, *In Place of Strife.* The title, to appeal to the Bevanites, suitably echoed the title of Nye Bevan's one and only book, *In Place of Fear,* which was a rambling hotchpotch of insubstantial political notions. It was mild enough stuff. A large helping of the Government's proposals were devoted to strengthening the unions and to making it more difficult for employers to sack inefficient workers and to other devices to upgrade union power.

But there was a tiny bit of daring in it, too. There was to be a twenty-eight-day conciliation pause in unofficial strikes and in strikes not preceded by adequate discussion, during which the unions were to be obliged to get their members back to work while attempts were made to persuade them to go through accepted disputes procedures and to reach a settlement. If strikers disobeyed the order to return to work they could be proceeded against in the civil courts and presumably fined or otherwise dealt with if they defied the courts.

In national strikes the relevant Minister was to be given power, after consultation with union leaders, to order a ballot to find out whether union members actually wanted to go on strike. There was to be a Commission on Industrial Relations. It was to aim at reforming industrial relations and would deal with sticky problems. Most weight was put in the proposals on the need to prevent unofficial strikes which were claimed to be responsible for ninety-five per cent of the strikes in Britain.

When the White Paper was debated in Parliament over fifty Labour M.P.s voted against it and others abstained. Naturally most of those who voted against the Government were of the extreme Left. They had the advantage of being able to make themselves seem respectable by being joined in the lobby by Liberal M.P.s. The greatly respected Social Democrat, Douglas Houghton, just dismissed from the Government, also voted against. From inside the Cabinet, James Callaghan, looking for the support of the union leaders in the future, disloyally let it be known publicly that he, too, was against trade-union reform. The extreme Left element in the Parliamentary Labour Party knew they were on to a good thing. They guessed that the Social Democrats and the Social Democratic leadership of the Labour Party would probably cave in to the further detriment of the Social Democratic cause.

The Left Wing, the union leaders and some who were not so Left Wing huffed and puffed through the early summer.

For a while it looked as though Wilson would hold firm. As late as mid-April he said, 'The Bill we are discussing tonight is an essential Bill. Essential to our economic recovery. Essential to the balance of payments. Essential to full employment. It is an essential component of ensuring the economic success of the Government. . . . That is why I have to tell you that the passage of this Bill is essential to its continuance in office. There can be no going back on that. . . .' From anyone other than Wilson this would have seemed a firm commitment. Connoisseurs noticed that in the same statement he had put in a fuzzy escape clause.

'We have told the T.U.C. on many occasions that if they would come forward with their own measures, equally effective, equally urgent in time, to our proposals to deal with unofficial strikes we would be prepared to consider their alternative suggestions.'

By mid-June Custer's Last Stand was over, though it is fair to note that Wilson and Barbara Castle held out alone till the last. Wilson then announced in the House of Commons that the General Council of the T.U.C. had 'Unanimously agreed to a solemn and binding undertaking which set out the lines on which the General Council will intervene in serious unconstitutional stoppages. In the light of this undertaking, the Government now regard the T.U.C.'s proposals as satisfactory. . . . In these circumstances, the Government have decided not to proceed with proposals for legislation involving financial penalties for those involved in inter-union and unconstitutional disputes.'

The 'solemn and binding undertaking' of the T.U.C. was, of course, a farce. In the passage of time it disappeared and it has never been effective against unofficial strikes. The twenty-eight-day conciliation pause which Wilson had said was vital to the Government's continued existence vanished. So did the power of the relevant Minister to order a strike ballot in cases where the national economy could be seriously affected.

Wilson lamely pretended that the T.U.C.'s alternative proposals were sufficient, knowing they came nowhere near the Bill which he had described as 'essential to our economic recovery'. Wilson was not entirely to be blamed for losing his nerve. The rest of the Cabinet, alarmed by the noises of the trade-union leaders, had turned and fled, with the exception of Barbara Castle. Though priding herself as being very much on the Left, in office she had the honesty to recognize what needed to be done and with feminine practicality had set out to do it.

June 1969 marked the final surrender of the leadership of the Parliamentary Labour Party to the trade-union leaders' block votes. The extreme Left were jubilant. They saw the significance of the Government's defeat. It meant more than a permanent veto by the T.U.C. General Council on Labour legislation which it did not like. It presaged the imminent arrival of the actual dictation of policy to the Labour Party and to Labour Governments.

The Social Democrats in the Cabinet who had run away justified their pusillanimity. They claimed it as an inconsequential concession to the T.U.C. in return for their continued adherence to the Government's Prices and Incomes policy. If it was a defeat they saw it as a tactical defeat in a skirmish, not as it really was — a massacre in a battle which ended a war. Extra-Parliamentary forces had been influential in the Parliamentary Labour Party before but hitherto they had not dominated it as they were now about to.

In the run-up to the general election the trade-union leaders and their extremist associates in the Parliamentary Labour Party did not assert their authority too openly. That would have been bad electorally. If the trade-union leaders had been democratically elected and representative of their member's views the defeat of the Parliamentary Party leadership would have been of less consequence to Social Democracy. If those with the great block votes in their hands had been staunchly Social Democratic the relationship between Labour Governments and the trade-union leaders would have been that of like-minded partners and not that between master and servant.

Probably, the fact that the public were dimly aware that far from being put down the trade-union leaders had been elevated was a cause of Labour's defeat in the general

87

election of June 1970. But it was not immediately apparent that the Social Democrats had been massively devalued. Roy Jenkins had successfully solved the balance-of-payments problem and manoeuvred the country towards the restoration of some of its economic health. To those who stood at a distance from it the Labour Government in 1970 did not look bad. I cannot pretend that I fully comprehended at the time that Social Democracy in the Labour Party had been so seriously and lastingly undermined that it was unlikely to be rebuilt. But I knew a terrible thing had been done.

When in June 1969 at the Parliamentary Labour Party meeting Wilson typically announced his defeat as a victory there was jubilation. While the others applauded the reconciliation with the big brothers outside Parliament whom they feared so much I felt sick in my stomach. I was on the verge of getting up to say that Wilson had just announced that Labour would lose the next election but the meeting closed without any discussion. I wish now that I had been a little braver, not that it would have done any good.

CHAPTER EIGHT

Wilson's Appeasement and the Feebleness of the Social Democrats consolidate the Hold of the small ultra-Left

THERE WAS not enough time between capture of the commanding heights of the Labour Party by the trade-union leaders and the 1970 election for them to use their enhanced power to reshape Labour's election manifesto. Nor, probably, had they yet formulated in their own minds what new postures they would impose upon the Labour Party in collaboration with their extremist friends in the Parliamentary Labour Party. At any rate the election manifesto was comparatively harmless. Much attention in Labour propaganda was concentrated on Labour's achievement (which now has an old world charm about it) in turning the £800 million balance-of-payments deficit it had inherited in 1964 into a surplus of £600 million.

There was nothing in Labour's 1970 election manifesto about fresh major nationalization. There was talk of strengthening the nationalized industries and allowing them to do things hitherto prohibited. There was waffle about helping cooperative enterprises. There was the usual bromide about how marvellous Labour would be for industry. Threats to wreck private enterprise were decidedly muted. There was no proposal for a wealth tax. I had no difficulty in supporting the manifesto.

It is possible, though in retrospect unlikely because of the new subordination to the union leaders, that if Labour had won the 1970 election it would have produced a fairly good Government. That was my view as I stood as a candidate. I was worried by the underlying trends but still had sufficient optimism to believe that the Social Democrats could fight back and restore their old authority in the Party. Certainly Social Democracy in the Labour Party would have had a better future if Labour had won. The Conservative victory brought on the eclipse more rapidly.

There were two reasons for this. The Common Market and the Conservatives' own Industrial Relations Act.

As Prime Minister, Wilson, with the full authority of the Labour Cabinet and the Parliamentary Labour Party, had applied to join the European Economic Community. Wilson was a total convert. His enthusiasm rose to a height which alarmed even fervent pro-marketeers. He would not take No for an answer, he declared.

But in Opposition it was different. The union block votes were against us joining the Common Market. The leaders who cast their union block votes were completely indifferent to the views of their members who were overwhelmingly in favour of British entry as they showed in the 1975 referendum. But the union leaders, particularly those on the extreme Left like Jack Jones and Hugh Scanlon, had grasped the implications of the trouncing they gave Wilson over his proposals to reform the unions. They knew now that their orders would be obeyed. They were supported by all the extremists whether among lower-placed trade union officials or in the constituency parties or in the Parliamentary Labour Party.

The raucousness was deafening. When it was added to the quieter arguments of genuine Social Democrats with sincere misgivings about the Common Market it all became too much for Wilson. He feared that if he kept to the policy he had followed as Prime Minister the Labour Party might split and that he might lose the Leadership. He hid among the conditions which must be fulfilled before Britain joined. With degrading grovelling to the Left and to the anti-Marketeers he sought to make his previous enthusiasm look as though it had merely been an exploration to find out whether or not quite ridiculous conditions would be accepted by the Common Market as the price for British entry.

When Heath achieved entry Wilson said that he would

never have accepted the conditions. This was convincingly refuted by George Thomson (now Lord Thomson of Monifieth) who had been the Minister in charge of negotiations under Wilson. He said that on the contrary Wilson and the Labour Government would have been delighted to accept the same conditions as those on which the Heath Government acceded to the Treaty of Rome. As he was fully in Wilson's confidence at the relevant time his evidence is decisive.

The Social Democrats were split. Those in the Parliamentary Labour Party who remained true to what Labour declared as its policy in office were deserted by many Social Democrats who normally would have sided with them. And some of the Social Democrats who joined with the extreme Left Wing over the Common Market did so because of the congenital lack of courage from which British Social Democrats suffer. Not all the defecting Social Democrats were so rabid against the Common Market that, in the absence of Left Wing pressure, they would have been willing to withdraw the help they had once given in the Commons voting lobbies to Wilson's application to join.

This is another difficulty in maintaining Social Democratic influence in the Labour Party. Too many of the Social Democrats collapse under stress. They do not care to be pilloried in their constituencies. They have the example of Dick Taverne as a terrible warning. After he voted in favour of Common Market entry in 1971 he was disowned by his Party in Lincoln. Though, after resigning, he won a by-election in 1973 as a Democratic Labour candidate and held Lincoln again in February 1974, his political career was finished. Social Democrats fear the strength and energy of their local Left Wing which could force their premature retirement by a successful demand for the selection of a new candidate. The Left Wing are rarely disunited. They remain a coherent fighting force. The Social Democrats are easily scattered.

After the general election of 1970 Roy Jenkins was elected Deputy Leader of the Parliamentary Labour Party. That was a favourable sign for Social Democracy. But the gain was soon to be obliterated.

The National Executive of the Labour Party over the two years 1970–2 had as its Chairman the ultra-Left Wing Ian Mikardo. The Vice-Chairman was Wedgwood Benn, eagerly currying favour with the extreme Left Wingers. Like Wilson before him he sought their support to make him eventually the Leader of the Labour Party. All save Denis Healey among the National Executive members chosen by the constituency organizations section were extreme Left Wingers. Three of the five women members of the National Executive were likewise.

This was a very sure indication of the shift of view among the trade-union leaders. It was their block vote which put the three ultra-Left Wing ladies on the National Executive whereas in earlier years they would have had no chance of election. By now the whole tilt of the National Executive was very Leftwards and dominated from outside by the union leaders with the largest block votes.

This National Executive was happy to work with the extremists in the Parliamentary Labour Party to produce a denunciation of the Labour Government's pledges on the Common Market. They saw the dreadful position which the Social Democrats would be in. To be true to the old official policy they would have to oppose the new official policy.

Another weakness of the Social Democrats is that they very much dislike having to oppose official policy. It is more comfortable for them, if they have to defy their extreme Left Wing enemies, if they can say they are doing so from loyalty to official policy of the Labour Party. Now everything was upside down. In the autumn of 1971 the Parliamentary Labour Party imposed a three-line whip to force all to vote against British entry into the Common Market. Sixty-nine Labour M.P.s, Social Democrats to a man, and a woman, defied that order. Thus British entry was carried with the aid of a substantial number of Labour M.P.s. But that sixty-nine comprised only about half of those in the Parliamentary Labour Party who were not extremists. The Social Democrats were in a sorry mess.

By general consent the leader of the Social Democrats in the Parliamentary Labour Party was Roy Jenkins. He had long believed strongly in British membership of the

Common Market. The reversal of the previous official policy put him in an impossible position. He did not feel able to continue to vote against Conservative legislation to complete the formalities for British entry because it would be to deny his deeply held and well known beliefs. He could not continue to support an official Labour Party policy which turned upside down the carefully thought out policy of the old Labour Government. The breaking-point was reached when, after he had been re-elected Deputy leader, the Party officially changed its position by demanding that Parliament's decision to enter the Common Market should be subject to a subsequent referendum. Consequently he resigned the Deputy Leadership and the Social Democrats were greatly weakened thereby.

The Conservative Government's Industrial Relations Act was similar in many respects to that proposed by the previous Labour Government in the White Paper, *In Place of Strife*. It was not particularly sensible but there was no great harm in it except for the consequences it brought. What both the Labour Government and the Conservative Government were trying to do in their efforts to reform the trade unions and curb their power was to deal with the new situation caused by the arrival at the top of the trade unions of extremists whose main concern was the destruction of society rather than its improvement.

No one would have thought of introducing legislation to curb the powers of the old leaders like Ernest Bevin, Arthur Deakin, Tom Williamson, Bill Carron, Jack Cooper and the like. They fought for their members' interests within the terms of a democratic society whose citizens could only be prosperous if industry were not disrupted. In time leaders of this kind would have come round to reforming the trade-union structure themselves or, in so far as legislation was needed to help to this end, would have done so in amiable cooperation with a Labour or Conservative Government.

The way to ensure we get sensible trade-union leaders who are Social Democrats, or democratic in outlook, is to see that union members are able to elect them unhindered. Both the Labour Government of 1964–70 and the succeeding

Conservative Government missed a great opportunity. The process of reform of trade unions should have begun by ensuring some more or less uniform standard of democracy within the unions.

The Electricians' Union has had, since it got rid of the Communist crooks, a postal ballot of all its members for important Executive positions. This has kept the leadership of the union in safe Social Democratic hands. The reason is that when all the members of a union can vote quietly at home in a secret ballot counted by an impartial outside body (in the Electricians' case the Electoral Reform Society) they will not usually vote for extremists. Naturally a few extremists who are outstandingly efficient as trade-union officials will get elected but not in sufficient numbers to force the unions into political stances disapproved of by the members as a whole.

Since the Engineers' Union has had the postal-ballot system there has been a transformation in the composition of the Executive Council. The Engineers' system is not perfect because the votes are not sent out and returned for counting by an independent body like the Electoral Reform Society. They are sent out by and returned to the union itself for counting and this system always allows the possibility of malpractices by the malevolent.

Again, the supreme policy-making body of the Engineers is the National Committee. This has fifty-two members from the twenty-six divisional committees which each have the right to send two delegates to the National Committee. The divisional committees are composed of those who have been elected by members of the district committees. In turn those district committees have been elected in part by shop stewards and in part by branch members. But, and it is a very big but, there is no postal ballot involved and a vote can only be cast by the ordinary union member if he attends the place where the vote is being conducted. Such is the disinclination of the average person to take part in democratic activities if he is put to the slightest trouble in so doing that very few union members actually cast their votes to decide who shall be members of the district committees. This leaves a way open for the dedicated extremists to

94

ensure that the elections to the district committees are won by fellow extremists.

Accordingly the National Committee of the Engineers' Union does not represent the views of the ordinary members. In 1977 at least twenty of its fifty-two members were ultra-Left Wing, either being actual Communists, or sympathizers, or advocating views on the far Left. Five wobble about from one side to another. Only twenty-seven are solid Social Democrats. This gives a very narrow majority for common sense, and in many years there is not even that narrow majority.

In the Transport and General Workers' Union there is no postal ballot for the General Secretary who is elected for life. The permanence of his position gives him unassailable power. The General Executive Council, not elected by a postal ballot, meets every two or three months though its Finance and General Purpose Committee meets monthly. All other officials, apart from the General Secretary, are appointed by the General Executive Council and not elected. The General Secretary is obviously in a very strong position to see that the officials appointed are all to his way of thinking.

The General Executive Council could give the General Secretary some trouble but usually does not because of the dominance which the General Secretary is able to achieve. Though all members have the right to vote for members of the General Executive Council they must attend the proper places for voting to exercise that right. This allows the extreme Left to win a disproportionate number of seats on the General Executive Council. Usually there are ten or eleven very Left Wing members out of the thirty-nine.

This would suggest that out of the 1,900,000 membership of the Transport and General Workers' Union nearly half a million have extremist views on politics and would be quite happy with the state of affairs that exists in Eastern Europe. But obviously there are nothing like half a million members of the Transport and General Workers' Union holding extreme Left Wing views. But there may well be half a million who vote Conservative. They have no representation on the General Executive Council whatever.

By their approach to trade-union legislation the Labour and Conservative Governments gave the chance to the unrepresentative trade-union leaders to pose as defenders of trade-union democracy and of the trade unions' right to run their own organizations free of outside interference. What they should have done was to have had a short Act of Parliament, which in the climate of the times could have been passed, setting out a system of voting on important issues and for important officials in the trade unions by postal ballot to be paid for by the Government and conducted by an independent body.

It would have been very difficult for the union leaders to refuse the offer of democratic procedures provided free. As their stock-in-trade is to prate about industrial democracy and greater democracy for the workers it would have been hard going for them to defend a position in which their members cannot fully exercise democratic rights within their union and to refuse to allow them to do so.

Maybe the opportunity will come again to ensure that the unions are democratic and it should not be missed when it does. But now we have the absurd situation in which trade-union leaders can call for greater industrial democracy through Bullock-type participation in the boardroom while nobody dares point out that they are denying democracy to their own members. The reason that they deny it is obvious: many trade-union leaders would be smoked out once their members began to vote in large numbers and particularly if they were required, as they should be required by law, to state their politics in their election addresses. As I have previously explained, Communists and other extremists are very reluctant when standing in union elections to give any indication of their far Left politics because they know this would greatly reduce their chances of election.

Nevertheless the Tories might have got away with their trade-union legislation had it not been for the opening it gave to the Communists and their allies which they seized upon. Ordinary rank-and-file members of the unions were not at all put out by the minor restraints placed upon their leaders. The common-sense trade-union leader was not unduly worried either. But the weaker of the trade-union leaders were very susceptible to taunts that they were lacking in will to resist a capitalist Government's so-called threats to the liberties of trade unions. The anti-Social Democrats among the union leaders were agog to resist and to be seen as valiant for the battle.

It was thus easy for a curious body called the Liaison Committee for the Defence of Trade Unions to whip up support for disobedience to the Industrial Relations Act. That Liaison Committee was dominated by the Communists who supplied its drive and its operational planning. Gradually the feeble-minded were persuaded that the trade unions were under threat of extinction. The T.U.C. was stirred into hostility against the Government. The period of what came to be called confrontation had begun. However, it was not the Conservative Government who confronted the unions but the other way round.

The importance of this was the further weakening of the Social Democratic position. Social Democrats must believe in obedience to laws passed by elected governments. They must further believe in the right of such governments to introduce legislation they think fitting, and without having that legislation defied by important sections. If a Conservative Government are not to have their laws obeyed because small groups of dissidents don't like them, the need to obey the laws of a Labour Government is equally questionable. If democratic decisions are to be ignored by minority strong-arm groups of the noisy then it is that much harder for the views of the Social Democrats in the Labour Party to prevail even though the great majority of Labour voters agree with them.

The Labour Opposition should have denounced the numerous breaches of the law stimulated by the Liaison Committee for the Defence of Trade Unions. It did not because too many Labour M.P.s, as well as their leaders, were anxious not to provoke the extreme Left but preferred to seem sympathetic to them.

When the National Union of Mineworkers decided on an overtime ban in November 1973 to force the Government to concede wage increases not allowed by stage three of the Government's legally enacted prices and incomes policy there was no call from the Opposition leaders to obey the law. When the overtime ban turned into a strike there was still no condemnation. Though it must be conceded that when Mick McGahey, the Communist vice-chairman of the N.U.M., said that the strike was designed to bring the Conservative Government down and that the miners should appeal to the troops not to move coal if they were ordered to do so Wilson did take some action. He tabled a motion in the Commons, signed by 114 Labour M.P.s repudiating McGahey's attitude. But the damage had been done. Nor did Wilson seek to have his motion debated. That would have obliged him to condemn the miners' strike.

The first 1974 election was fought upon the issue of who governs Britain – the unions or the Government. The official Labour Party had made its stance clear. It was not the elected Government which should prevail but the voice of the unions however unrepresentatively expressed by their leaders.

The Labour Party's period of Opposition from 1970 to 1974 was the worst up till then for the Social Democrats. Wilson, a weak and trimming leader, did not try to contain the undemocratic elements. To give in to them made open splits in the Labour Party less probable. The Social Democrats did not have the courage to fight back with any great vigour. They felt helpless without the official machinery behind them and that had passed over to the Left. The Party conferences and the National Executive and Transport House itself were no longer controlled by the Social Democrats. They had the support of all but five to ten per cent of Labour voters but they did not know how to use it and were frightened to appeal to the great mass of Labour voters for help in frustrating the anti-Social Democrats.

They feared that if they pushed their opposition too hard the Labour Party would be split and that they would be left stranded without funds or an organizational apparatus on which to base either a new Social Democratic Labour Party or a claim to be the true Labour Party. Thus the claim of a few union leaders elected by undemocratic procedures to speak for the Labour Party was conceded. It was established because unrepresentative leaders in alliance with the extremists of the far Left of the Labour Party, in turn sustained by the vociferous minorities in the constituency parties, were able to foist on the Labour Party, with the use of the block vote, any policy of their choosing.

Since the elements who had seized the fundamental power in the Labour Party were extremists it was obvious that they would seek to make the Labour Party's official policy as far to the Left as they could, consistent with the public not understanding clearly what it meant and not being brought to disenchantment with Labour candidates. Marxists want a Marxist state. Between 1970 and 1974 the Marxists' philosophy came into command of the Labour Party's thinking. The only check upon them was that the leaders of the Parliamentary Labour Party must agree to any election manifesto. But those leaders are hard put to keep out of it anything which has been passed by the Party conference.

They know that the Marxists will never be satisfied without some fresh pieces of nationalization being included in the manifesto. Unfortunately the Conservatives had not denationalized steel so this ground did not have to be gone over again. What was the least the Marxists and the ultra-Left Wing would be satisfied with in 1974? Shipbuilding, ship repairing, the aircraft industry, ports, sections of pharmaceuticals, road haulage, construction and machine tools were chosen. Perhaps the public ownership of ports is not too serious a matter though those which have remained in private hands have a far better record in profitability and efficiency than the publicly owned ports.

But nationalizing the aircraft and shipbuilding industries will be seriously damaging to the economy. It means that shipbuilding will be propped up however bad that might be for the national economy. It means risking that the aircraft industry, accustomed to exporting hundreds of millions of pounds worth of product every year and to making a substantial profit, will become a nationalized loss-maker. The leaders of the Parliamentary Labour Party were aware of this but could not think of any other sops less damaging to offer to the extremists.

Fortunately Parliamentary time has prevented the

inroads planned on the other industries. But the assaults are merely postponed until Labour has a larger majority.

Labour's manifesto for February 1974 said, 'The graver our economic situation the more important it will be to protect the poorer groups of the community – such as the pensioners – by drastic redistribution of wealth and income.'

This presaged not only raising the existing tax system to even more penal levels but making additions, 'We shall introduce an annual wealth tax on the rich; bring in a new tax on major transfers of personal wealth . . .'

Those who understood economics among Social Democrats in leading positions in the Parliamentary Labour Party knew all this to be nonsense. It has again and again been demonstrated that if every penny of income to all individuals over £10,000 a year were confiscated the amount of redistribution possible would only give those below £10,000 a year a few pence a head. And since, in those circumstances, salaries above £10,000 a year would not be paid, much of that potential for redistribution would disappear. Similarly if all substantial fortunes and large houses were confiscated by the State the wealth of the average person, and the poor, would not be increased. Taxation has for long been so high on so many that the amount of further redistribution possible is minimal. The only result of turning the screws further is to provide a powerful disincentive to people to create wealth or to make more money. This reduces the general wealth available in the country for redistribution and makes the poor poorer.

One of the aims in the Labour manifesto of February 1974 was 'To achieve far greater economic equality – in income, wealth and living standards'. Another was 'To increase social equality by giving far greater importance to full employment, education, housing and social benefits'. A third was 'To bring about a fundamental and irreversible shift in the balance of power and wealth in favour of working people and their families'.

Such aims were dramatically ambitious and the Social Democrats knew that they would require a vast increase in public expenditure. It would have to be paid for by general

100

taxation, the inflationary printing of money and huge borrowings abroad. But the extremists either did not recognize this or did not care. Their aim was to create a rigid society entirely controlled by themselves and the bureaucrats, with a low standard of living in which all would be equally downtrodden.

They also had, and have, another aim in view. The larger the government payroll can be made the greater the voting strength for Labour. Labour is the champion of public expenditure however wasteful. The waste includes having unnecessarily swollen staffs whether in the Civil Service, the town hall or such organizations as the National Health Service. Labour, extremists and Social Democrats included, is able to say quite truthfully that the jobs of these employees are safe so long as there is a Labour Government but are threatened if there is a Conservative Government.

The numbers game in payroll employees is becoming increasingly significant. In June 1976 there were some 2,900,000 local-government employees. That was an increase of around 400,000 since 1971. It was an increase of 1,200,000 over the figure for June 1964 when we had only 1,700,000 local-government workers. In April 1976 there were 747,000 civil servants employed by the central government. That was nearly 50,000 more than in 1971.

There are some 850,000 workers in the National Health Service. About 450,000 are dentists, nurses, midwives, doctors and other technical staff. The rest are administrative, clerical, porters, cleaners and other ancillary workers. Their numbers have multiplied exceedingly without any improvement in the quality of the National Health Service. In the opinion of many qualified to judge the standards have gone down as the employees have increased.

Add the totals employed in the Civil Service, local government and National Health Service alone. They come to approximately 4,500,000. When wives and adult dependents are included the voting figure at general elections is gigantic.

By the nature of their work none of these employees can be connected to a profit motive or have any direct interest in whether industry does well or badly. They get their pay and their increases just the same. If we could get the numbers in this area down to the figure we had in 1964 the savings in public expenditure would be in the area of £6,000,000,000 a year. The scope for tax reduction and diversion of resources to productive industry would be terrific. But the Labour Party, particularly the extremists, are desperately concerned that this should not happen. It would mean a tremendous loss of votes to Labour at general elections among those who are aware that Labour is more likely to keep them in comfortable unexacting jobs than the Conservatives are.

The extremist is not concerned about getting value for money in the public service by using only that amount of labour required to do a job effectively and organizing the work so that productivity is increased. The extremist is committed to wasteful public expenditure for the very reason that it increases or maintains the number of people dependent on central and local government wastefulness. It is a device for making more and more people dependent upon State patronage, of which the best guarantor is the Labour Party.

An added attraction to the extremist is that this wasteful expenditure entails an unnaturally high rate of taxation. It enables him to say that in order that justice should be done those with incomes beyond £10,000 a year and with assets beyond £50,000 should be annihilated by taxation. This levelling down provides surface justification for high rates of taxation on the rest. The desirability of this is that the more the ordinary person is forced to pay in tax the less he has left to spend according to his own choice. This makes him more reliant for the amenities of life on what the government, national or local, decide to provide for him. He may not want a minute share in a sauna bath, a golf course, or a swimming pool but by heavens he will have one. He may not want to subsidize unproductive jobs in dying industries but he will. The less money the individual is allowed to keep the less democratic expression can he give to his wishes and the more he becomes a slave to the State; and eventually he accepts his fate because he can see no way of escaping it.

Too many of the Social Democrats fail to denounce wasteful public spending because they cannot distinguish between the actual spending and the results obtained from it. They are afraid to examine public spending closely for fear that they will be labelled as lacking in compassion and in zealotry for egalitarianism. It should be obvious, but it is not, that public money spent wisely to relieve suffering, to improve health, education, housing and equality of opportunity does good. But when public money is spent sloppily without regard to economy or general usefulness it does harm.

All Labour Governments have begun by overspending and have been forced to draw back. Each time they have drawn back the protests of their Left Wing have become more influential and the cutbacks less effective. Each Labour Government leaves us with a total of public spending higher than when it took office and which weighs down productive industry still further. By uneven jerks the economy grows weaker.

CHAPTER NINE

The Marxist Minority in the Labour Party controls the Minority Labour Government

BY 1974 I could not have stood with a clear conscience as a Labour candidate even if there had been an opportunity. The drift to the extreme Left had gone too far and the weakness of the Social Democrats was too great to resist it. They got most of the top places in the Labour Governments which followed but at the cost of accepting policies with which they did not agree. They were the front men for the extremists in the constituency parties, among the trade-union leaders and in the Parliamentary Labour Party.

Britain has had minority governments before. But she never had a minority government which did not act according to the majority views of that government, and those who voted for it, but along the lines dictated by a minority within the party ostensibly supporting the government.

The Labour Party got 37.2 per cent of the votes cast in February 1974 and 39.3 per cent of the votes cast in October 1974. On both occasions less than 30 per cent of the potential electorate voted for it. Labour's percentage of the actual votes cast when it *lost* the election in 1970 was 43 per cent – substantially higher than when it *won* the largest number of seats in the House of Commons twice in 1974. But this did not inhibit Labour from embarking on a far more Left Wing programme than it did after the 1966 general election when Labour got 47.8 per cent of the votes cast. (Labour could conceivably have said then that if the 24 per cent who did not vote at the 1966 election had voted then sufficient of their votes would have gone to Labour to give them over 50 per cent of the country's support.)

But now Britain was to see why the capturing of key positions by fanatical minorities in constituency Labour Parties and in the unions was of more than parochial interest. The country has not yet fully understood the meaning of this though the evidence is remorselessly unfolding. There is the union block vote represented by unrepresentative union leaders at Labour Party conferences, on the National Executive of the Labour Party, and in consultations with a Labour Government. That block vote is used in a way which reflects the views of an almost infinitesimal number of union leaders and not those of the millions of members in whose name it is used. It is the basis of minority power posing as majority power in the Labour Party. Allied to it, each feeding upon the other, is the power of the very Left Wing in the constituency parties. Labour Party membership in 1977 has shrunk to 445,000 instead of the claimed 695,000 according to a Gallup Poll broadcast by B.B.C. 'Panorama' on 8 March 1977. At one time Labour Party membership was well over a million.

Interest in management and executive committee meetings of local Labour Parties' meetings is at zero and attendance and willingness to serve on them and to undertake the chores necessary to run them is minimal. As at trade-union branch meetings, the determined far Left Wingers, acting in concert with a few others, can seize and operate the policy-making functions. Threatened from outside by the block vote of the union leaders and from inside by incipient revolution from his local constituency Party upon whom he depends for continuance as the official Labour candidate, the Labour M.P. has for the most part become a wretched creature. He thinks in one way but the strings manipulated by his masters turn him into a puppet facing in another direction.

The Labour M.P., whether a back-bencher or in government, is constrained to act not in the public interest but in that of his own need to survive. A danger in this process is that, forced to say what they do not believe, otherwise reasonable Labour M.P.s come to believe what

105

they are saying. From resisting the measures advanced by the far Left they become advocates of them to keep their self-respect. The road towards Eastern Europe becomes ever more difficult to retrace. Thus the minority within the minority tightens its strangling grip.

It would be surprising if more than seven or eight per cent of the population, including the workers in the industries concerned, wanted the nationalization of aircraft and shipbuilding and even they would not have been worried if it had never taken place. The proportion among Labour voters, taken separately, in favour of more nationalization is scarcely higher. Yet the ultra-Left said it must be done and done it was with neither economic nor democratic justification. It was a necessary part of the ultra-Left Wing plan to engulf the nation with profitless industry subsidized by the individual taxpayer. With aircraft and shipbuilding safely nationalized the next move can be made to take over further chunks. The State thus extends its area of employment and the dependence of its employees upon the government so securing their lives, their souls and their votes. That the general standard of living goes down, or does not rise as it might, is secondary to the importance in the extremists' minds of subordinating everyone to the bureaucratic machine.

Depressing the standard of living actually helps the extremist. When wage restraint becomes unavoidable he talks of the sacrifices made by the workers though the people he is talking about have suffered relatively far less than the rest of the population. The demand is then made for real sacrifices from the enterprising, diligent and those who choose to spend their money as they and not the State please. The spirit of envy is invoked and in times when prosperity is not rising it is a powerful agent though the people it is invoked against have higher social consciences than average and bear the heaviest real cuts.

There was no mention in the Labour Party manifesto for the February 1974 election of the abolition of pay beds but it did say that Labour would 'Phase out private practice from the hospital services'. By October the screw had turned and the manifesto was stating that Labour would 'Phase out

106

private pay beds from the National Health Service'. In the preceding months the spirit of envy had been hard at work.

Ignorant louts in hospital workers' unions led by extremists insisted that pay beds should be ended. There was no sense in it. The beds were not needed for ordinary National Health Service patients and there were not enough private clinics to accommodate those willing to pay. The threat of losing a valuable part of their income accelerated emigration among the ablest and the youngest doctors. There was total disregard of the fact that payment by private patients made a substantial contribution to the National Health Service and that those private patients paid twice over because they had given up their entitlement to free beds. There was total disregard, too, of the right of the individual to choose how to spend his money. It was conceded that he might spend as much as he liked on beer, tobacco, the football pools and gambling of all kinds but he must not spend money on getting a degree of privacy in hospital or on taking out an insurance to provide it for him. The spirit of envy demanded the abolition of pay beds as another step towards the Eastern European condition. At the same time planning difficulties were put in the way of those anxious to build private clinics. One more freedom was listed for extinction.

As was to be expected, the passion for expenditure by the government, unmatched by increased output or productivity, led to new excesses in the printing of money by the Labour Government, and to disastrous inflation. The union leaders, fortified by their ultra-Left Wing notions, ordered the Government not to make any substantial reduction in Government expenditure. But they did offer to limit wage increases if the Government complied with rules they laid down for trying to do so.

In July 1975 came the White Paper, *The Attack on Inflation*. In its preamble the Government explained that the rules were to be as adumbrated in the T.U.C. document contained in the White Paper. The pretence that the Government had made the policy and not the T.U.C. was completely abandoned. The policy was designed largely by Jack Jones of the Transport and General Workers' Union.

Despite his apparent mildness he is very Left Wing in his views. He and his extremist friends saw the chance for a new impetus towards an Eastern European society. Those with incomes of £8,500 or over were to get nothing. With increased taxation and inflation running at twenty-six per cent they would hence be savagely impoverished, discouraged and demoralized. Differentials between the creators of wealth and the managers of industry and those who work and make a living as a direct result of their enterprise and skill would be further diminished.

Originally the Government said that a £6 flat-rate increase, or ten per cent up to £300 allowed to the lowest earners, was to be a limit and not an entitlement. Lionel Murray, General Secretary of the T.U.C., and Jack Jones quickly contradicted the Government. They decreed that the Government were wrong and that the ten per cent or £6 flat-rate increase was an entitlement. This was despite the truthful Government declaration in the White Paper that many firms would not be able to afford the £6 limit. Employees who did not receive it were instructed to complain to Murray who would arrange for them to get it. The T.U.C. was appointed by the Government as the umpire and arbiter in all matters concerned with the Government's pay policy.

Large numbers of workers who would not in the ordinary way have received as much as £6 extra accordingly got it. The general wage increase was consequently much higher than it need have been. This suited Jack Jones and his extremist allies very well. It guaranteed a continuation of inflation, though the Government when presenting the T.U.C. policy said that it would bring inflation down to a rate of ten per cent by the third quarter of 1976 and to single figures by the end of 1976. The very act of turning the £6 limit into an entitlement effectively prevented this. But, apart from that breach of the Government's policy, the situation really demanded that no one should have a wage or salary increase of any kind for at least a year so that serious inroads could be made on inflation.

Another great advantage to Jack Jones and the extremists was that the £6 flat rate meant that everybody under £8,500 a year was limited to a £300-a-year increase. Consequently the differentials between skilled workers on, say, £3,500 to £6,000 a year and lower-paid workers on £30 to £50 a week were unacceptably eroded.

The inevitable effect of this was that the levelling down of the skilled workers was greatly resented by them, creating tensions within industry which were to slow down its capacity to recover, and tensions in society which would damage its structure. The Leyland toolmakers' strike in February and March 1977 illustrated the point precisely.

The extremists did very well out of the Social Contract composed by the Left Wing trade-union leaders. Those at the top end of the incomes scale were punished for the sins of government overspending for which they could not possibly be blamed. Skilled workers, junior and middle management, were reduced to a level closer to those whom their role is to inspire and to direct and suffered a calamitous cut in their standard of living. The multitude at the bottom end had their situation actually improved to begin with and even when things got worse continued to incur the least cut in their standard of living.

They were not to know that the Social Contract, by allowing the continuation of government overspending (which could only be maintained by borrowing from abroad and at home because even the penal taxation extorted was insufficient to support it), was certain to bring about vast unemployment. This was accentuated by the collapse or reduction in size of many firms unable to afford the £6 limit without corresponding increases in production.

Why the Social Contract should have been regarded as a success is baffling. Inflation in March 1977, on a three-monthly basis, was still running at twenty-one per cent. Average earnings since its inception have gone up by more than double the agreed percentages.

Nevertheless a further dose of this Marxist policy was ordered in August 1976. Once again the differentials were eroded by allowing £2.50 a week for all those earning up to £50 a week but limiting any rises for those between £50 and £80 a week to five per cent. This created a maximum of £4 a week which could not be exceeded however high the earnings above £80 a week.

An incomes policy related to increased productivity and higher rewards for higher skills and effort is very desirable – if the difficulties of making everyone accept it as just can be overcome. An incomes policy aimed at giving the least skilled and the least industrious a higher proportionate rise than those without whose determination and willingness to work long and creative hours (often with no overtime pay) there would be no industry, is an engine for Marxism. It puts in motion a perpetual demand from the multitudinous unskilled (including the least hardworking) to be paid more than the economic condition of the country can support. And to be kept permanently closer to the living standards of those immediately above them in the industrial hierarchy. The spirit of envy is given respectability. The hardworking and the skilled have been brought down by the Social Contract and it will be very hard to go against this trend in raising them up again.

It may be asked why the Communists opposed the Social Contract and the Labour Government's pay policies from 1975 onwards since they produced such favourable results for extremists. The answer is that the unrestrained public expenditure which the Far Left and the Communists demand would, combined with unrestrained wage increases, make prices and unemployment rise even faster. Discontent would mount more sharply and the destruction of industry and society would come more quickly. Jack Jones and his extremist friends preferred to drive on the road to Eastern Europe rather in more orderly style. That was in case miseries and hardships might be increased so fast that they would be blamed on their true originators – the Left Wing trade-union leaders and their extremist associates. If that happened they might never get to Eastern Europe. Nor is it offensive to say that this is their intended destination. According to the B.B.C.'s overseas monitoring service, Jack Jones himself said on East German radio on 26 June 1976 that he felt at home in East Germany. There is no reason to doubt him.

It might have been understandable if the Labour Government had surrendered its authority to the members of trade unions. At least they are nearly half the employees of the country. Their monopolistic control of Labour in a number of central industries gives them the power to halt those industries. Like all monopolies they restrict the supply of their commodity, which in this instance is labour, in order to charge more for it than if it were in plentiful supply. Accordingly we have had the unexpected situation in which there has been abnormal inflation, low output and productivity, and ever-rising wages accompanied by high unemployment reaching nearly one and a half million in June 1977.

Clearly, the trade unions are too important for the Government not to consult with them and to seek their cooperation. But the Labour Government of 1974 did not surrender to the views and attitudes of ordinary trade-union members but to the trade-union leaders, for the most part unrepresentative of their members. It is not the trade unions as such which have been elevated to alarming and disproportionate power in society but a minority of leaders ranging in their outlook from the Left Wing of the Labour Party to the ultra-Left and into and beyond the Communist Party.

Since 1974 the various policy-making bodies of the Labour Party have been dominated by them and their allies in the Parliamentary Labour Party. The takeover by the ultra-Left which was begun when Labout lost the 1951 election and resisted and even turned back for a while by Hugh Gaitskell has proceeded to completion.

Labour's Programme for Britain 1976, published in May 1976, sets out the plan for creating an Eastern European style society in Britain. At the 1976 Labour Party Conference at Blackpool care was taken to see that this plan was endorsed by a card vote. It would easily have passed on a show of hands but the card vote was necessary so that it could be recorded that the policy was endorsed by a two-thirds majority. This makes the whole document of 147 pages the confirmed and actual policy of the Labour Party.

The card vote in favour of *Labour's Programme for Britain 1976* showed 5,833,000 in favour and 122,000

111

against. It is impossible to say that the policy does not have the almost unanimous backing of those who control the Labour Party. As an addition to the document, which was first published on 28 May 1976, Labour's National Executive issued a further statement on banking and finance for endorsement by the Labour Party conference. This additional National Executive statement announced the impending nationalization of the four big banks — National Westminster, Lloyds, Barclays and Midland. It committed Labour to taking over the seven largest insurance companies. It also declared that Labour would take over at least one merchant bank. This National Executive statement was also put to a card vote so that it could have the required two-thirds majority and become official Labour Party policy. It was carried by 3,314,000 votes to 526,000.

Callaghan vainly tried to stop the National Executive statement on banking and insurance becoming official Labour policy. Yet, despite his assertion that he would not allow this nationalization of banking and finance to go into the next election manifesto, the Labour Party conference took no notice. The block votes wielded by the ultra-Left Wing unrepresentative trade-union leaders have now ensured that one day a Labour Government will carry out this nationalization. It may not be the next Labour Government, but the remorseless push of the Marxists and their friends will ensure that if it is not the next Labour Government then the one after will do the job.

Callaghan had the courage to stand out against the nationalization of banking and the large insurance companies. He dared not oppose the endorsement of *Labour's Programme for Britain 1976*. He said, 'I very much welcome *Labour's Programme for Britain 1976*. It has involved the work of hundreds of volunteers, as well as members of the N.E.C. and our hardworking staff at Transport House. . . . To be successful it will require mutual respect, mutual trust, a recognition of our differing roles and our separate responsibilities. That is my desire and it is in that spirit that I invite the National Executive to join us in planning ahead.'

112

There could not be a clearer commitment to put *Labour's Programme for Britain 1976* into practice. True, the N.E.C. admits that doing so would take more than one Parliament. But it will be regarded as a manifesto and a mandate for the next Labour Government and their successors. The Social Democrats as well as the Marxists are committed to it. The Social Democrats put up no fight. By 1976 they had given up hope. There is no need for the Communists to win representation in Parliament so long as this programme remains official Labour policy. It goes further than the demands of Continental Communist Parties and echoes those of the British Communist Party. Already Britain has a far larger nationalized sector than Sweden or West Germany where the Social Democratic Governments have sensibly relied on free enterprise to produce the wealth for general prosperity and redistribution.

In Britain, the nationalized industries account for thirty per cent of those employed in industry. This is apart from the four and a half million employed in central and local government and the National Health Service. *Labour's Programme for Britain 1976* would put nearly half the population employed in industry under nationalized boards. (In 1965 only twenty-two per cent of the working population were in the nationalized industries.)

We would cease to have a mixed economy. It would be an economy dominated by the nationalized industries. Nor should it be assumed that having achieved *Labour's Programme for Britain 1976* the Marxists would be satisfied. They would go on and on until clause four had been turned into a reality by a State takeover of all but the smallest businesses.

No area is to be left alone. Many of the famous names of industry are marked for destruction. Burmah Oil, Allied Breweries, Unilever, Cadbury, Wimpey, Taylor Woodrow, Laing, Richard Costain, Associated Fisheries, Plesseys, The London Brick Company and so on. Naturally, all land is to be nationalized and forestry and pharmaceuticals and plant hire and other industries are to be invaded.

The extension in bureaucracy would be immense. Labour plans new armies of civil servants. They would have to man

113

a new National Planning Commission. This body of civil servants would be required to tell all industry, not merely that which has been nationalized, what to do and how to invest. Just as in Eastern European countries the government would make the plans for industry and order industries to carry them out however unsuitable they may be for the economy. Strangled by regulations and inappropriate instructions, what was left of free enterprise would be bankrupted and thus could be taken over by the Marxist-dominated Labour Party at little cost until the State owned everything however profitless and inefficient it had become.

Is it unfair to say that the Labour Party is Marxist dominated and is set upon a course indistinguishable from Communism? Norman Atkinson, Treasurer of the Labour Party and elected by the combined votes of the trade unions and the constituency parties, does not think so, 'The Labour Party still remains a Marxist party. It has said so. Its aims and objectives are clearly set out in its Constitution, and all the leading Labour names . . . accept the Labour Party's Marxist Constitution.'

Dissent from this assertion is not possible after reading *Labour's Programme for Britain 1976*. Every aspect of life in industry will have its government-appointed commission entrusted with the powers and responsibility of implementing the Marxist State. Added to the National Enterprise Board there will be an Investment Bank. There will be an Agricultural Land Commission; new Regional Authorities with great powers of direction; a Cooperative Development Agency to promote workers' cooperatives such as the disastrous (until rescued by G.E.C.) Meriden motor cycle venture and the collapsed *Scottish Daily News* workers' cooperative. This last agency will be empowered to provide experts and money to any wishing to establish similar madcap schemes.

The present Foreign Exchange Control Committee will be 'Transformed into a specialized unit able to take account of all the facts of inward and outward investment'. The intention is obvious. It is to restrict British investment overseas however much more profitable it may be to the economy in certain circumstances than investing in Britain.

The country is to proliferate with committees and commissions interfering with productive industry and ensuring that all industries down to the most remote and unimportant are forced into the Marxist straitjacket. Local authorities are to join in the fun. They are to be encouraged 'To undertake a range of industrial and commercial activities'.

Naturally, the Bullock Committee's recommendation that half the boards of companies employing more than 2,000 people should be appointed by the trade unions is endorsed. This last is part of the Marxist strategy to try to control decision-making in industry by undemocratic means whether there is a Labour Government or not. The T.U.C. has been persuaded to demand that employee directors should not be voted upon by all the employees in the firm concerned whether they are in unions or not. If all workers voted members of junior, middle and sometimes even senior managements would win seats on the Board. Being sensible people who understand what industry is all about they would support top management's decisions, however painful, which were necessary to increase prosperity and thus the survival of the firm.

The object of the T.U.C. is that the employee directors should be appointed by the trade unions and need not even work in the place concerned. As is customary in all positions connected with trade unions the majority of the posts would go to the most extreme.

The Marxists know that the more extreme the employee directors the more damage will be done to industry. The trade-union-appointed directors would fight the giving of high rewards and incentives to senior management without which good management cannot be obtained. They would insist on distributing the profits principally by way of higher wages and give nothing to the risk takers and little for the buying of modern equipment. They would be aided in this by the natural inclination of shopfloor employees to think in the short term and not in the long term, to think that the extra £5 a week immediately is more attractive than an extra £2.50 with the other £2.50 being used for modernization which would make all jobs safer and eventually lead to a higher increase in wages than the immediate £5.

Union-appointed directors would discourage all management attempts to reduce restrictive practices. They would be uninterested in knowing that our industrial competitors use two men on machines on which we are obliged by the unions to use three men. The union-appointed directors would, in union terms, be highly conservative. They would be anxious to continue demarcation lines and to hang on to every impediment now preventing the most useful employment of labour by management. They would always be on the side of caving in to demands backed by threats of strikes. The extremists would know very well how to tap the conservatism among trade unionists in support of their overall plan to disrupt British industry. British industry having been utterly brought down would then be ripe for nationalization with low compensation, thus enlarging Marxism in the State.

Some of the T.U.C. backers of parity in the boardroom may sincerely believe that it would be helpful to industry in gaining greater cooperation between management and employees. For that reason some Communists are opposed to the idea, feeling that the trade-union-appointed directors would be suborned by management. But with many extremists among them, including those with Trotskyist and other extremist views, there would be no danger of that.

Basically the idea is to give more power to the extremists, who will not be representative of the ordinary trade-union member, in ruining British industry.

That power would be retained when there was a Conservative Government and would be stronger when there was a Labour Government. The shareholders' representatives on the board, who would be drawn from senior management, would be forced to compromise with notions they knew to be very harmful in order to get anything done at all. It is said that this system works well in Western Germany. But it is not the same system.

For Britain it is proposed that there should be one board only. In Germany there is a supervisory board which makes general decisions. Below it there is a normal board which manages the firm on commercial lines. In Germany the employee directors on the supervisory board are elected by all members of the firm concerned whether in a union or not and must, unlike in the proposal for Britain, work at the firm. Among those employee representatives there must be at least one who is a member of management immediately below the top flight. In case of deadlock he is most likely to go along with the management view which he would have helped to shape.

Again, in West Germany there have been works councils for many years out of which employee participation on supervisor boards has evolved. In Britain the unions have successfully thwarted works councils, save in a few instances. The unions have wished to retain the right to give their version of what is happening to union members rather than to allow management to explain the facts. This leads to distorted and inaccurate information being given to the employees which enables the extremists to get the backing of the shopfloor because the management case is never fairly put.

Perhaps the most important difference between West Germany and Britain is that in West Germany the unions believe in making profits. They actually own commercial undertakings including a bank. A major cause of West German prosperity has been the belief of employees at every level that profits are good for them – and they have been. In Britain, where the Labour Party and the union leaders are infected by Marxism, decades of propaganda have made profits synonymous with exploitation. The theory is that what profits there are should be at once wrested from the entrepreneur primarily responsible for them and distributed in immediate pay awards without thought for future investment.

The trade-union leaders have created a state of mind among their members by which profits are held to be sinful. Managements have been driven to defend profits instead of extolling them. The cutting edge has been taken off their drive to make profits for fear of difficulties with the trade unions. With half the boards of companies employing more than two thousand manned by trade-union appointees,

117

many of whom would be extremists, the attempt to make profits would be still further frustrated.

Another device under the disguise of industrial democracy by which to exert extremist influence and control, notwithstanding the wishes of the electorate, is that contained in the notion that local-council employees should have seats on council committees and on the council itself as of right. The Labour Party set up a joint working party with the T.U.C. under the chairmanship of the General Secretary of the National and Local Government Officers' Association. Their declaration of policy was endorsed by the General Council of the T.U.C. and the Labour Party National Executive on 23 February 1977. It demands that the law be changed to allow representatives of local authority workers to be non-voting members on Council committees. The representatives are to be elected by the trade unionists only, with a minimum of two representatives but allowing for one-fifth of each committee to be so appointed. The declaration asserts, 'However, the existing position of teachers co-opted, *with* voting rights, on to Education Committees should be maintained.'

The same document demands that employees be represented with voting rights on 'The managing and governing bodies of schools, colleges, etc.' Again, they must be union members and elected by the trade unionists alone. Nor is the employee representation to be confined to teachers. Non-teaching staff are to have their voting rights as well. This presumably covers caretakers, cleaners, school-meal servers and the like. Those most willing to sit on the governing bodies as employee representatives will usually be those with the most extreme views. The system will be another handy way of determining policy, this time in the sensitive educational area, in a Marxist direction.

Since the Labour Party National Executive and the General Council of the T.U.C. issued their demands on 23 February 1977 there has been a further development. The National and Local Government Officers' Association, whose General Secretary acted as Chairman of the T.U.C–Labour Party working party, have made a further demand. They insist that the trade-union appointees to local-council committees should have voting rights and that there should be at least four trade-union nominees on the full local council, also with voting rights. The fact that none of these would have been voted upon by the electorate in council elections and that therefore the democratic rights of the voters would be thereby diminished is ignored by the T.U.C., the Labour Party and NALGO. The last also demand that local-government employees should be able to stand for election in local-council elections. This, added to the unelected employees, would give local-government employees as much influence as, if not more, than councillors not employed by the local authority.

NALGO also propose similar worker involvement in the National Health Service, the universities, electricity, gas, water and transport industries and in the running of industrial estates and new towns. The argument that NALGO present is that joint control between management and workers of overall decisions affecting working lives is the true purpose of industrial democracy – a doctrine which pays no regard to the interest of the consumer or the people for whom the services are designed.

It is easy to brush all this aside with the comfortable feeling that it will never come to pass. It is easy, but it would be an illusion. Once the T.U.C. and the Labour Party have agreed upon a course then a Labour Government is certain to implement it. It would be very difficult for a Conservative Government to backtrack and make good the genuine democracy that had been lost.

CHAPTER TEN

Further Demonstrations that *Labour's Programme for Britain 1976* is the road to Eastern Europe

EVER EAGER to open the door to the Kremlin the Marxists have secured a commitment in *Labour's Programme for Britain 1976* to a massive reduction in our defence by additional defence cuts. The cuts are to be at least £1,000 million a year at 1974 prices. As the Marxists intend, this would end any effective contribution which Britain could make to NATO.

On top of that Labour is committed to ending British exports of arms. This loss of exports coupled with the cut in arms supplied to the British forces would lose some 400,000 workers their jobs but the Marxists would prefer them to be unemployed than to remain engaged in their wicked activities. *Labour's Programme for Britain 1976* regards with dismay, not pleasure the fact that 'As an exporter of arms Britain is now second only to the two superpowers.'

The parts of *Labour's Programme for Britain 1976* dealing with British foreign relations could have been dictated direct from the Kremlin. Marxist Cuba is praised. Brazil and Chile are condemned. Association with any regime not approved of by the British Marxists is to be curtailed or ended. Particular disapproval is registered against Saudi Arabia and Iran without whose help our economic condition in the mid-seventies would have been still worse.

Naturally *Labour's Programme for Britain 1976* advertises further penal taxation, 'A great deal remains to be done to bring in more income tax revenue . . .' A wealth tax is urgently demanded rising to five per cent a year on assets held. It will not be long before no one is able to accumulate more than the £50,000 which individuals are to be allowed to hold without being subject to a wealth tax. But even this does not go far enough for the Marxists: 'Tax requirements and increased public spending, though making society less unequal, will not be enough in themselves to bring about the massive redistribution of wealth we seek. We believe it is essential to set targets for the redistribution of income and wealth and to establish a firm programme for meeting them.' We are well on the way to implementing fully the doctrine that all should be paid the same and that there should be no incentive or reward for greater efforts and higher skills and enterprise.

Nor is the Press excluded from coercion. There are nasty little hints of censorship and control ahead. Advertising revenue is to be pooled so that the more popular newspapers can be forced, by having large parts of their advertising revenue confiscated, to support unpopular newspapers. There is to be a fund out of which new publications can be financed. There is to be a newsprint subsidy to be given to allow the less popular and more extreme newspapers to be subsidized. There is to be a tax on advertising.

Labour's recent evidence to the Royal Commission on the Press remarked, 'Eventually we could achieve a situation where no distinction was made between readers in terms of class, wealth and spending behaviour. By eliminating the intervening influence of the advertiser, and ultimately rendering each Press consumer of equal advertising value, the Advertising Revenue Board' (to be set up by a future Labour Government) 'would help to make the Press more accountable to the general public and more representative of the broad spectrum of interests in society.'

To make sure that very Left Wing policies prevail there is the pronouncement: 'We believe that industrial democracy lies at the heart of any acceptable scheme for long-term reform of the Press. The situations and possible solutions will vary from paper to paper and might, therefore, range from full co-ownership to a supervisory board model composed of management and worker representatives.' The worker representatives would of course be chosen by the

121

trade unions and would consist largely of the ultra-Left agitators who have almost wrecked Fleet Street and who would insist on the policy of their newspapers being little different from that of the Communist *Morning Star*.

There is no excuse for anyone not to understand what the Labour Party intends to do about the Press. In a resolution passed by the Labour Party conference of 1975 it was additionally declared that the newsprint subsidy to aid small-circulation papers would be conditional upon agreed forms of worker participation and that the money provided for new publications would only be given if the publication were 'Managed democratically on a cooperative basis by all those employed on the publication'.

To complete the threat to the freedom of the Press the resolution also stated that the National Print Corporation which would be set up to provide subsidized printing to publications with editorial views acceptable to a Labour administration would also have 'Powers to bring existing printing plant into public ownership'.

There is no doubt that a Labour Government will one day seek to implement this and other means to cow the Press. The Marxists know very well that it is impossible to run a Marxist State if a free press continues to operate within it. The repression which is inseparable from a Marxist State requires that the citizen should not know the facts about what is going on in his own country or abroad. It requires that the citizen should have no place, other than in controlled Party circles, to voice any criticism of the way the country is being run. Isolation from fact and opinion is essential in curbing discontent and refusal to cooperate with the authorities. It is not by chance that as the Marxist influence has grown in the Labour Party so has concern with ways, which it is hoped can be made to look respectable, to end the freedom of the Press.

These strange suggestions for controlling the Press in the interests of the Marxists and the ultra-Left are not the frothings of a minority unlikely to get power. The minority has demonstrated that it has very real power over the Labour Government and Labour policies. What they say has to be taken very seriously if freedom is not to be lost by accident. Hitler obligingly set out his plans in *Mein Kampf* but the world did not read this instructive work for fear of being bored. The Marxist extremists controlling the Labour Party have with equal frankness set out their plans. It is not witch-hunting to point out the similarities of their ideas to the systems operating in Eastern Europe. It is merely recording the facts from their own published proposals.

Nor is it alarmist to remind ourselves that the capacity of the leaders of the Labour Party to resist the encroachments of the Left has steadily lessened since Hugh Gaitskell's death. Most Social Democrats in the Parliamentary Labour Party would start by pooh-poohing the possibility of *Labour's Programme for Britain 1976* being enacted. But on reflection they must be bound to concede that there is no way of stopping it. The trade-union leaders not only control the crucial block votes at Labour Party conferences: they provide ninety per cent of the funds needed to keep the Labour Party going. If their demands are not met by the Social Democrats in the Parliamentary Labour Party leadership they will find ways to throw them out and replace them by ultra-Left M.P.s. In this they would have the vociferous support of the constituency Labour Parties.

Already the Labour Party is on its way to changing the method of electing the Leader and Prime Minister. At the 1976 Labour Party Conference a resolution was passed instructing 'The National Executive Committee to establish a working party to define the Office of Leader of the Labour Party and report within one year on the procedures for Leadership elections. This working party shall be especially charged to consider appropriate means of widening the electorate involved in the choice of the Leader.'

This resolution should be read in conjunction with the resolution passed in the previous year. It demanded 'That the Leader and Cabinet of the Parliamentary Labour Party should be elected annually by Conference'. To which there was an amendment which read that 'The Party's candidate for the Premiership or Leader of the Opposition and a Deputy should be chosen by Conference in advance of each General Election, that appointments to other offices should be made on a more democratic basis. . . .'

The intention is manifest. A Michael Foot or a Wedgwood Benn or an Ian Mikardo cannot get elected by the Parliamentary Labour Party to the Leadership. But it is exactly that kind of person who would be elected by the Party Conference. The Social Democrats know that once the right to choose the Leader is taken from the Parliamentary Labour Party they are doomed.

But will they succeed in defeating this move? It is very much in the mood of wider participation and industrial democracy now preached by the very Left whenever they see some gain to themselves from it. The very Left are against postal ballots in the unions because these would displace their friends. They are against all employees, whether unionized or not, being allowed to vote to choose which employee directors they would like to see on the boards of their companies if such an arrangement is instituted. Widening the area of selection of such directors out of control of the extremists could mean that elected employee directors might actually add something of value to their firm and not engage in disrupting it.

The Labour Party conference is exactly the kind of unrepresentative group which extremists like to have. On paper it sounds democratic but in practice it is not. The constituency Party delegates are elected by the tiny number who control the local constituency Parties and which are now much influenced by the extremists. They do not in any way represent the majority view of Labour voters. Likewise, as we have seen, the trade-union leaders delivering the block vote deliver it in accordance with their own opinions which have now become very Left Wing. How very satisfactory to be able to record, when a resolution has been passed or a Leader has been elected, that it has been done by millions of votes when those millions of votes are just pieces of paper manipulated by the few who have possession of them.

Once the new system of election of Leader comes into operation a Wedgwood Benn, an Eric Heffer, a Frank Allaun or a Judith Hart or someone worse of whom we have not yet heard could be elected Leader. The orthodox Social Democratic leaders will bow still further in obeisance to the Party conference and be the more willing to carry out its dictates. Either way Social Democracy will be totally routed.

With the National Executive Committee of the Labour Party firmly in the hands of the extremists it is not surprising that during 1975 and 1976 it produced a spate of resolutions attacking the Labour Government which remained too moderate for it despite its craven appeasement of the extremists. In July 1976, for example, it attacked the Government for announcing its intentions to reduce slightly the amount of increase originally planned in public spending. And one of its resolutions was almost comic. It deplored the Government's White Paper on public expenditure as being 'In direct conflict with the election pledge of "a fundamental and irreversible shift in the balance of wealth and power in favour of working people and their families"'.

The composers of the resolution seemed to overlook the elementary fact that continuation of overspending by the Government could not be financed by the so-called rich sufficiently to avoid the working people being made to suffer ruinous taxation as well.

Fully to realize the Marxist leanings of the Labour Party N.E.C. a look at its resolutions on foreign policy, supplementing *Labour's Programme for Britain 1976,* is rewarding. The governments of Spain, Indonesia, Brazil, Dominica, and South Africa are frequently condemned for repressive action. The governments of Soviet Russia and Marxist States are never similarly condemned. If they are mentioned at all it is with sycophancy and, by implication, with praise. On 10 February 1976 the National Executive deplored the failure of Western governments (including the British Labour Government) to support the Marxist M.P.L.A. in Angola. 'So they turned to the Soviet bloc for help.' They did indeed and with the help of Cuban soldiers established a Communist dictatorship which meets with the approval of Labour's National Executive.

During a period when the Labour Government repeatedly sought and got financial assistance from America, West Germany and other Western industrial democracies it might have been supposed that a brief word

125

of thanks would occasionally appear in statements by Labour's National Executive. Perhaps an expression of solidarity with democratic nations anxious to rescue a country brought low economically by the extravagance of a Labour Government obeying the orders of the trade-union leaders and the National Executive might have crept in. After all, the Labour Government would have collapsed during 1975, 1976 and 1977 if the International Monetary Fund had not helped. But to acknowledge that help had come from countries which are rich because they believe in, and practise, free enterprise vigorously would make *Labour's Programme for Britain 1976* look ridiculous. None of the countries whose aid the Labour Government so frequently call upon would regard *Labour's Programme for Britain 1976* as other than the dangerous Marxist nonsense that it is. If they understood how near it was to fruition they would be very reluctant to continue with their loans and help.

All in all, *Labour's Programme for Britain 1976* is a chilling document. Its object is to give the State ever more power. Not merely by nationalizing more industry, though that is part of the plan as Wedgwood Benn indicated when he remarked at the Brighton Labour Party Conference in 1971, 'We want industry to be in the public sector to change the power structure of our society.'

Labour's Programme for Britain 1976 is a Marxist and Trotskyist plan to extend the power of the State to a detailed control of the individual's activities. Seizing the main banks and insurance companies will assist in this by regulating what the individual can get by way of credit. The National Planning Commission will, under Government direction, issue comprehensive orders to all industry whether nationalized or not. Those firms still allowed to remain in a free enterprise condition will be clobbered by the Government if they do not do as they are told.

Public spending is to be increased. The tyranny of the bureaucrat is to be extended and encouraged. The resultant greater inefficiency is thought by the Marxists to be of no consequence. They do not mind, for instance, that in 1966 there was one administrator for every 9.5 hospital beds and that by 1976 there was one administrator for every 4.8 beds. Employing more than are necessary concentrates more power in the hands of the State, increases public spending and creates a larger payroll vote.

As I have said, the aim is to leave the individual with nothing besides a little pocket money which he may be allowed to spend on cigarettes, drink, motoring and going to football matches. From year to year the State will decide how much he will be left with to enjoy these fripperies. The bulk of his income will be devoted to supplying inefficient and wasteful mass social services, many of which could be obtained by other means far more cheaply.

Indeed, in the 1977 Budget debate, Alex Lyon, a Labour M.P. with Social Democratic pretensions, actually said, 'The policy has always been to provide for the standard of living out of public expenditure, leaving the ordinary wage earner to provide out of his wage packet only the less essential parts of his standard of living.'

What is the point of this desire of the Marxists and their allies to concentrate more and more power in the hands of the State? It can have nothing to do with democracy. Civil servants and other bureaucrats are not elected and do not become more democratic by having trade-union appointees forced on them. Ministers and their Governments are elected. But it is impossible for the general voting public to exercise detailed control over their activities. The more power that Ministers have got over more matters the less easy it is to exercise any kind of control at all. The issues are too varied and too complex for any but a few specialists devoting their whole time to one out of a myriad of subjects to understand.

The purpose cannot be to improve the standard of living. The evidence is too strong in showing that the greater the degree of nationalization and bureaucratic control the greater the loss in output and productivity.

There can only be one purpose for accumulating huge powers for the State. It is to give satisfaction to those who enjoy exercising those powers. Hypocritically, they claim to act in the name of the State in response to the wishes of the people and for the benefit of the people but these power mad men have no means of discovering what the people's wishes are or if they do they ignore them if their views are contrary to their own. They have no intention of allowing the State to wither away. They confidently believe themselves to be the State and whatever shreds of idealism they begin with are rapidly corrupted away by power.

It would seem unthinkable that the Marxists and Trotskyists and ultra-Left Wing fanatics should be able to foist their ideas on the British people. But in the same speech in which Callaghan welcomed *Labour's Programme for Britain 1976* he said, 'I also draw the Party's attention to a new factor creeping into the Party, which I warn against – namely those elements which misuse the word "Socialist" and who seek to infiltrate our Party and use it to their own ends. They are almost all recognizable by their jargon and their intolerance. . . . The main bulwark against these infiltrators is a strong and active membership in every constituency for these people represent only a small group. But I do suggest to the National Executive Committee that they would do well to examine these activities, see what is going on and report back to the Party.'

Shortly after that appeal to the National Executive to halt the takeover by the extremists the Labour Party National Executive appointed an avowed Trotskyite to be Youth Officer of the Labour Party. The National Executive, being in the hands of extremists, is naturally hostile to a Labour Prime Minister's suggestion that they should be got rid of. And when the report asked for by Callaghan was received in May 1977 the National Executive found it so damaging that it resolved that it should not be published and should not even be sent to the members of the National Executive, who could view it only on application.

Trotskyists do not believe in Parliamentary democracy. Referring to the German Social Democrat Party, Trotsky wrote that it did not

Bind itself to bring the masses to Socialism *only* through the gates of democracy. In adapting ourselves to the Parliamentary regime, we stopped at a theoretical exposure of democracy, because we were still too weak to

128

overcome it in practice. But the path of Socialist ideas which is visible through all deviations, and even betrayals, foreshadows no other outcome but this: to throw democracy aside and replace it by the mechanism of the proletariat.

No rubbish about Parliamentary democracy for Trotsky or for his followers who preach today the revolutionary and violent road to Socialism accompanied by the armed seizure of State power. And these are the views of those now highly influential in Labour policy-making.

During the Attlee Government of 1945 to 1951 it seemed unlikely that those on the very Left would ever come to dominate the Labour Party. But they did. It might seem unlikely that so comprehensive a Marxist approach as *Labour's Programme for Britain 1976* could ever be enacted by a Labour Government. But it will be, if we are too bored by politics to follow what is happening and to prevent it. We can be lulled into supine readiness for the kill by temporary delays in the advance of Marxism.

It was not a turn towards moderation which prevented Labour completing the 1974 manifesto. It was the failure in their Parliamentary majority. The wealth tax, the nationalization of ports, of ship repairing, of profitable firms in pharmaceuticals, in road haulage, in construction, in machine tools, were just postponed to await a better majority. Then a handsome start can also be made on *Labour's Programme for Britain 1976.*

If I am right about the steady advance towards a Marxist or Eastern European style State, how is it that most of us are unaware of the danger to freedom and the hope of prosperity? Because it happens so gradually. The change is not being made after a *coup d'état,* a revolution or a civil war.

For example, Britain's industrial decline relative to the performance of other industrial countries has been spread over a long period. There is no single day on which it could be said that this is the day when Britain sank below other industrial nations. The decline was too slow to be vividly noticeable and was masked by other events.

The Industrial Revolution made Britain pre-eminent

among the manufacturers. It was inevitable that other nations with similar intelligence and sufficient raw materials would catch up with us. We could not keep our industrial secrets. Exported machinery could be readily copied. British firms were happy to assist foreign firms in establishing counterpart factories. An extraordinary burst of industrial genius had put the British ahead. Foreigners were bound to want to find out how it had happened and to stimulate their own industries.

As her industrial decline began Britain was actually getting increased benefits from her huge overseas investments. Her Empire, in which she devoted much sincere attention to the interests of the inhabitants, also brought advantages. In many parts of the Empire it was for a long time impossible to import goods unless they came from Britain. Many colonies would have in any case bought British to a large extent because British expatriates were responsible for much of the importing. The Empire did not collapse on one day: it weakened and expired over decades.

There were two world wars which for various reasons made it difficult for the British to keep up with their competitor nations. In the last world war West Germany and Japan had the good fortune to be defeated by democracies led by the U.S.A. In West Germany much of the machinery which had been destroyed was replaced by the most modern equipment with American aid. In Japan the advance into becoming one of the great industrial powers was also accelerated by American aid.

During Britain's industrial decline the general wealth of the world, particularly that of the industrial countries, has been rising. New technologies, improved machinery leading to higher output, and all the apparatus of industrialism have been pushing up general standards. That applies also to agriculture which has benefited everywhere from better methods of cultivation. It is absurd for the Kremlin to boast that the Russians are now better off than they were under the Tsars. It would have required bungling on a scale beyond even that of Communist inefficiency to prevent them so being. The Russians have been washed up higher by worldwide advances in industry and agriculture. The real

130

question is: would the Russians be much better off today if, like America and Western Europe, they had enjoyed a free-enterprise system since 1917? The answer must be that they would have been far better off. Under the Tsars their position relative to other countries with industrial potential was much higher than it is today.

In Britain something similar has been happening. The generality of people were better off after the First World War than they were before it. They were again better off after the Second World War than they were before it. This was not mainly due to conscious redistribution of income and wealth. That is only part of the answer. Britain benefited by post-war world shortages and increased output arising out of new technologies which were taking place all over the world.

The point is that if our industry had been better organized and our trade unions had been less obstructive in the operation of new machinery Britain's prosperity would be at a higher pitch than it is today and the ordinary people would be substantially better off. But the fact that they are in considerable degree better off masks the obvious proposition that they could have been still better off and obscures our industrial decline relative to our industrial competitors. If you have a colour television set whereas last year you only had a black and white television set you are less inclined to pay attention to the drop in the British share of the world markets.

Between 1974 and 1977 some awareness that things were not right economically did penetrate into the minds of the generality. They noticed that wasteful overspending by the Labour Government caused huge overseas borrowings and the printing of money to meet the Government requirements. The amount that could be collected in taxes even at the penal rates applied by the Labour Government were not sufficient to cover the gigantic public spending initiated and persisted in by that Government.

Everything feasible had been squeezed out of the better off and any attempts to get more would not remotely cover the gap. For example, if no one had to pay more than fifty per cent of his earnings in tax the loss to the Exchequer would be less than £200 million. A sum which is infinitesimal in the global figure of overspending. Taxation which rises to eighty-three per cent on earned income and ninety-eight per cent on unearned income is malevolence not intended seriously to raise revenue but intended to satisfy the disagreeable feelings of envy among the extremists.

But as the potential for getting more out of the above-average earners was exhausted the broad mass of the population had to be penalized by higher taxation as well. This was done to such an extent that, combined with the non-stop ever-higher rate of inflation stimulated by Government spending and printing of money, the standard of living actually began to fall in the latter half of 1976 and the first half of 1977. Until then Jack Jones' Social Contract which insisted on an uneconomic rise of around twenty per cent for millions had meant that only those in the middle and upper ranges of income had suffered acutely. When the rest began to suffer, too, they became aware that Britain's relative industrial decline was not a meaningless phrase but had real meaning. But it took a long time for the message to arrive, if it truly has yet.

However, the incipient realization of Britain's industrial decline, and hence her inability to grow more prosperous as fast as other industrial nations, will soon be forgotten when North Sea oil flows. The North Sea oil will not make us as prosperous as it would if we were not declining relatively as an industrial nation. But it will make us more prosperous than we are now so our industrial decline will once again be masked. Our gradual relative industrial decline will continue without much attention being paid to it, until it is too late, because of its gradualness. It is the same with the erosion of our freedoms by encroaching Marxism.

The proposed wealth tax, sometimes talked of as starting at £5,000 and sometimes at £100,000 worth of assets, does not seem too serious to the generality. Inflation will gradually make it seem more serious but so imperceptibly that there may be no revolt against it. The capital transfer tax which almost nullifies the right to give or leave money to your children is lessened in its impact as an attack on freedom because of the concomitant provision that a person may leave to his or her spouse all his or her property without any death duty. But if there is no surviving spouse, or when the surviving spouse dies, the capital transfer tax payable on death is horrific compared with other European Economic Community countries.

Official figures given in May 1977 show what happens when an estate passes to one son aged thirty without children in various countries. Suppose the estate is worth £300,000. In Britain the tax payable would be £144,750, in Belgium £39,106, in Denmark £53,022, in France £54,599, in Ireland £45,000, in Italy £34,723, in Luxembourg £23,975, in the Netherlands £46,636, in West Germany £30,591.

If the estate were worth £500,000 the comparable tax figures are: Britain £264,750, Belgium £73,106, Denmark £93,022, France £94,599, Ireland £137,500, Italy £81,134, Luxembourg £39,975, the Netherlands £80,636, West Germany £52,591.

Why do I use the word freedom in the context of taxation? Because all taxation is a limitation of an individual's rights to deal as he wishes with the money he has earned or accumulated. All taxation carried beyond a certain point must diminish the will, by effort and ingenuity, to earn more. For long this was recognized and care was taken not to raise taxation other than when it was essential for the security, survival or minimum well-being of the State. Slowly we have grown to accept the view that none of our money is our own, that the State owns all of it and is graciously pleased to allow us to spend an ever-smaller part of it. We are grateful for tax reliefs as though they were a present instead of a diminution in the amount confiscated. As I have already argued, the greater the taxation the less the liberty. Not only is the taxpayer made more dependent on the State but he has less freedom of choice as to what to do with his money. The decisions are increasingly removed from him, inducing a servile state of mind.

Penal taxes and actions in allied fields are not solely designed to make the generality subservient to the State. They are also aimed at destroying the confidence of, and annihilating, the natural leaders (other than political) in society. Taking away a man's right to charge interest on bank loans against his income tax is presented as an act of social justice. In fact it is intended to weaken the ability of top earners to accumulate capital. It also has the effect, because it is not selective, of hammering many quite ordinary people who have been encouraged to take out bank loans to help them with buying their house or motor car, and thus makes them still more dependent on the State.

The amount of revenue accruing to the State as a result of the 1974 Labour Government's limitation of income-tax relief on mortgage interest to mortgages of £25,000 or less, and to wipe out altogether tax relief on any second house or cottage in the country, was negligible. Its purpose was not to collect revenue but further to subdue and take away incentives from top earners. It was known very well to the members of the Labour Cabinet, including the limping Social Democrats among them, that the net effect would be yet another discouragement to the wealth creators to create wealth as they do in Japan, West Germany, France or America.

But an actual increase of total wealth in Britain is not an aim for the Marxists and their associates. The aim is to reduce step by step all to the same low level at which they can be more readily managed by politicians. Politicians, of course, receive their satisfaction in the wielding of power and from the self-delusion that they are serving the people when they are in practice for the most part massaging their own self importance. And the life of a Minister is agreeable with an official car and jolly dinners and luncheons at which he is able to make himself feel very important. True, some apparently die younger through overstrain but statistically there is no evidence that Ministers die earlier than those of corresponding responsibilities and burdens of work in the business world. Often overstrain on the Minister is caused by his inability to delegate.

The attack on private medicine is a part of the same approach. Uniformity of service and treatment as in Communist China makes the people more malleable to discipline from above. Labour politicians usually tend nowadays to claim that when they go into hospital they do so under strictly National Health Service conditions without using pay beds or any such privileged device by which they can supposedly jump the queue. But it is impossible for a Minister not to receive favoured treatment because he is not an ordinary person and officials cannot be brought to think of him as such. A sick Cabinet Minister is not put through the normal procedures affecting other people and however much his treatment may be called normal National Health Service treatment it is not.

Likewise the abolition of charitable status for public schools and grammar schools is not intended to raise revenue, which it wouldn't to any noticeable degree. It is intended as another humbling of those who seek to give their children the best education available. The existence of public schools and grammar schools is harmful in so far as it perpetuates class distinctions and assists in an undesirable ossification of society. But what is the higher earner to do about the education of his children? Every report which is published informs him that the standards of education in the State schools are declining and are likely to continue to decline.

The standards of morals in their widest sense in the State schools with their all-too-frequent lack of discipline and disinclination to concentrate on civic virtues are also declining under the influence of many ultra-Left Wing teachers who preach anarchy and the disruption of society. Until the top earner sees the State schools providing an education and attitude to life as good as that provided by the public schools and grammar schools why should he subject his children to them if he can avoid it? The Marxists believe he should be forced to by destroying the public schools and grammar schools which not only enable the top earner to get better education for his children but show up the poor quality of the education in the public sector.

Left Wing teachers in the comprehensive schools, to make sure that everybody is educated equally badly, insist that all children of the same age are taught in the same classes irrespective of the widely differing ranges of ability. They refuse to contemplate any relaxation of egalitarianism by allowing a streaming process according to which the

135

brighter children are able to move into different classes and progress unhampered by the less bright children. This in turn gives the less bright children a chance to acquire some self-confidence by not feeling inferior all the time. Thus in the name of a mythical and unattainable social justice the freedom of the individual to develop his own talents to the full is denied.

It is often asserted that the taxation imposed on the most active and industrious sections is no higher than that in comparable countries. This is in order to convince people that nothing very extraordinary is being done in Britain so what is all the fuss about? It is true that until recently taxation up to the £5,000 mark was not very much harsher in Britain than in comparable countries, though it is becoming so rapidly. But this deliberately overlooks a very important point. It is that salaries for jobs comparable to those in Britain are much more highly paid among our industrial competitors than they are here. A man on £10,000 a year in Britain would get well over £20,000 a year in West Germany, Belgium, Switzerland and the United States. He would get just under £20,000 a year in France, Canada and Sweden. An average family man in Britain on £10,000 a year is not left with much more than £6,000 after tax. The equivalent West German on £20,000 plus is left with some £14,000 a year. In Switzerland he is left with over £15,000 a year and so on.

I will put it another way. The maximum percentage rate of tax on earned income in Belgium is 63 per cent and from investment it is also 63 per cent. In Denmark the corresponding figures are 54.6 per cent and 70 per cent. In France 43.2 per cent and 60 per cent. In Germany 56 per cent and 56 per cent. In Luxembourg 57 per cent and 57 per cent. In Britain the maximum percentage rate of tax (all figures are for 1975) on earned income is 83 per cent and on investment income 98 per cent. In America no one has to pay more than 50 per cent in taxation. The inference from these figures is obvious when taken in context with the relative general prosperity of those countries and of Britain.

The inference is obvious, that is, except to the extremists who now control Labour Party policy. As we have seen they do not intend less taxation but more taxation for the British. That higher taxation will be directed with singular severity at the higher earners. In this, malevolence and envy as I have said are part of the motivation but the extremists, in so far as they are sincere, also think that squeezing the higher earners and the rich is socially just.

In an ideal world with plenty for everyone there might be some sense in decreeing roughly the same standard of living for all. There might then be no bar to a desire on the part of everyone to employ their talents usefully and to the full which would mean that everyone would cheerfully subordinate themselves to the State. Like devotees of a religion the populace would offer up their all, without thought of self, to the general good. Nationalized enterprises would all be profitable, and employees would work overtime when necessary without asking for overtime pay. No one would ask for a greater reward than the applause of his fellows. But such things could be only in a fantasy world which the extremists and the ultra-Left, when they are not simply being downright unpleasant, still imagine to be feasible.

In Russia the peasants have been allowed to keep one third of an acre to cultivate produce which they may sell at any price they can get in the open market. The land left for the private use of the peasants amounts to 1 per cent of the arable land of Russia. The other 99 per cent is farmed by the collective and state farms.

Yet the 1 per cent cultivated for private gain by the peasants produces one third of all the foodstuffs in Russia. If the Marxists were right the 1 per cent cultivated for private gain would not produce more than 1 per cent of the foodstuffs. They are not right, and the Soviet Government dare not confiscate the privately held 1 per cent of arable land for fear of even worse shortages than there are at present.

Indeed, elements of free enterprise are steadily creeping back into Soviet society. Car repairing, dry cleaning, the sale of luxury goods (even if not strictly lawful) are developing as major parts of the Soviet economy. While British extremists are trying to stamp out free enterprise the

Soviet authorities are reluctantly recognizing that the incentive it offers enables goods and services to be bought by the Russians which they could not otherwise obtain. Communist rule in sixty years has not been able to create a noble self-effacing society, and it never can.

Everything we know about human nature demonstrates that our extremists, however laudable their objectives, cannot succeed in achieving them. But still they will not believe it. Dedicated to the destruction of our society as it exists today the ultra-Left work hard. Personally, they are satisfied with the feelings of glory they acquire from working, often quite genuinely, for what they think is the good of the people.

The ultra-Left rightly point out that great scientists, writers, inventors, missionaries and nurses and many others with a deep sense of vocation do not do their jobs for money. Some do them because they are driven on by creative energy: others because they are sustained by a sincere wish to help the unfortunate or because they are content with giving loving service to their fellow human beings. There will always be a proportion of good and generous people in society who seek nothing for themselves, but there will never be enough of them to keep society prosperous, let alone make it more prosperous.

Consequently to act on the supposition that the great majority are selfless is immensely dangerous. The further that supposition is given legal shape the more difficult it is to prevent a material decline and to avoid dictatorial methods. Poverty cannot be eliminated this way. To help the weak we must help the strong and ambitious. Otherwise insufficient wealth is created to relieve the poor and deprived.

As less wealth is created as a result of destroying the incentive of the individual by penal taxation ever harsher measures have to be taken. Attempts to redistribute a decreasing amount of national wealth become more desperate. This drives away many who feel they could have a better life in other countries with fewer restrictions.

It is still possible to leave Britain, though if the Marxists get complete control it may become illegal as it is in East Germany and Russia and other countries with Communist regimes. As it is, growing restrictions have been placed on the export of capital to make it more difficult for the enterprising to emigrate. Britain has not yet implemented the provisions of the European Economic Community to allow free movement of capital between Britain and the other members of the Community.

Nevertheless Britons now emigrate at a rate well above 200,000 a year. Among technical and professional executives the rate of emigration rose from 32,600 in 1973 to 39,000 in 1974 and 59,000 in 1975 according to the latest figures at the time of writing. Penal taxation and the crushing of incentives by the Labour Government are driving some able and enterprising young people, and some in the prime of life, out of the country.

This is another reason for Britain's general industrial decline. Just as in horse breeding if the superior strains are removed the rest of the stock suffers. The very people who are prepared to take the risk of starting up afresh in a strange country are those whose attitude is most needed to revive British industry. But their going suits the Marxists very well for the time being. By diminishing freedom they push out many who are most attached to it in their personal lives. Those remaining, it is hoped, will accept being made creatures of the State and will eventually concur with the import banning, siege economy and limitation on the freedom of movement which will have to be imposed by the ultra-Left Wing if their style of Government is to be kept in being.

CHAPTER ELEVEN

The ultra-Left believes its Word is the Law

THE TRADE unions have been given privileges taking them outside the law a bit at a time. The bits are not so much at one time as immediately to impinge on our consciousness. Yet when a man has lost the right to sue trade-union leaders for persuading or compelling his employees to go on strike in breach of their contract of employment, particularly when he is not in dispute with those employees, he has lost a freedom. If the unions were in the weak state in which they originally began this might have been a reasonable price to pay to enable employees to oppose a grasping and unfair employer by the only means open to them – the withholding of their labour.

As it is, today employers and management are fearful of the unions and it is they who need protection to be able to carry on their businesses efficiently and profitably. In West Germany it is illegal to have a strike except at the expiry of a collective agreement after all the disputes procedures have been gone through. Even then there must be a secret strike ballot with a three-quarters majority to approve the strike. The German unions, keen as they are on profits, wholeheartedly concur with this law and regard strikes as only to be undertaken after protracted negotiation has failed to settle a dispute.

Consequently there have been only five major strikes in West Germany since the end of the war. The metalworkers' strike in the winter of 1956–7 in Schleswig-Holstein; the metalworkers' strike in Baden-Würtemberg in 1963; a freak

140

week of unofficial strikes in September 1969; the metalworkers' strike in Baden-Würtemberg in 1971. It is not surprising to learn that the metalworkers' union has an unusually Left Wing influence among its leadership.

The consequence of German restraint in strikes has been that while we lost 10,970,000 working days through strikes in 1970 West Germany lost 93,000 days. True, our strike record improved as unemployment grew in 1975–6, but it is now starting to return to previous levels with the unofficial strikes, such as those of the toolmakers at British Leyland in February–March 1977, of the maintenance engineers of British Airways in March–April 1977 and of the electricians at Port Talbot in April 1977, predominating. It is ironic to recall that it was the unofficial strikes which the legislation based on *In Place of Strife* was to be aimed at stopping and which the T.U.C. ordered the Labour Government to drop in return for a solemn and binding agreement that they would deal with and prevent unofficial strikes.

British employers and management for the most part have lost their freedom to arrange work in the way they judge to be most productive. In many instances the unions arrange the rotas of overtime however unsuitable the employees may be who are put forward to do the overtime. Often meal breaks are paid for by the employer at union insistence and in countless factories are not staggered so that machinery is idle and valuable production time is lost. The damage is augmented by the unavoidable delay in starting the machines up again. The management may not say how many men should be employed on a piece of equipment without union interference. The management may not say who will use that equipment: the union decides that.

When a majority of employees demand a closed shop the management must obey. That implies a loss of freedom not merely for managements but for millions who do not wish to join a union. They are forced into a union on pain of losing their jobs if they do not join. Should they offend the union in any way they can be and are expelled from that union and thus denied the means of making a living. If the management refuses to sack an employee who does not belong to a union where there is a closed shop, then a strike

141

automatically follows. But in West Germany the closed shop is illegal. Employees' wages are far higher than in Britain and so is profitability and general prosperity.

The phrase 'restrictive labour practices' is not translatable in to German. Such an amazing state of affairs is unknown there. Trade unions are not immune from normal legal processes as they are in Britain. Should there be a strike the State does not pay social-security benefits to strikers' families as we do in Britain. The union leaders themselves fear that if the State were to take over what should be financed by a union strike fund the authority of the union would be weakened. This would lead to power passing to the shopfloor away from the leadership and would give the Marxists the chance to initiate unofficial strikes. Unofficial and official strikes in Britain, of course, are bolstered by the State giving social-security benefits to the wives and children of strikers.

Naturally there is no fund available to pay employers who resist excessive wage demands which may be in breach of official pay codes to compensate them for loss of profits if they are so bold as to take on a union. This is another freedom lost to employers and managements who are obliged to fight the unions at a grave disadvantage and on unequal terms. The unions know that whereas the State will keep their members going a prolonged strike has every possibility of making the employers go bankrupt.

A further freedom taken away from the employer is his previous right to give notice to an unsatisfactory employee. That is to say, he may give such notice if he follows a cumbrous procedure taking many man-hours of the management. The employee may then challenge his dismissal at an industrial tribunal under the new Employment Protection Act passed by the 1974 Labour Government. Again many man-hours of senior management are lost to productive effort and assigned to defending the case, often lost because some minute part of the procedure has not been followed.

As it is known that the law is now biased heavily in favour of the employee it is anyway extremely hard to prove that the dismissal was reasonable. Many employers therefore put up with keeping on their payroll bad timekeepers and wantonly careless and idle employees. For the same reason they are becoming increasingly hesitant to take on new staff because of the difficulties of dismissing them however bad they may turn out to be. As the sanction of dismissal for poor workmanship has been virtually withdrawn, poor workmanship is on the increase. An additional barrier to slimming workforces to an economic size are the large redundancy payments an employer must pay by law to dismissed employees.

The legalization of the closed shop has another lost freedom implicit in it. The freedom of the Press is directly threatened. True, the management of a newspaper has to agree to the closed shop being introduced, giving it a right superior to that of the management of an ordinary business where a majority having demanded a closed shop and failed to get it, the union can appeal to A.C.A.S. which will rule in favour of the closed shop if it believes there is a majority who want it. The management will thus be compelled to give in.

Nevertheless, newspaper managements are very vulnerable to strikes if they don't give in. Though an editor is exempt from being compelled to join the union it is a little difficult for him to bring the newspaper out by himself if all the others are on strike. So far there has been little sign of the closed shop among journalists forcing newspapers to alter editorial policies. Only members of printing unions have sought to do that, as in 1977 when *The Times* was about to publish a précis of an article from another journal criticizing the restrictive and disruptive practices of printing operatives. Again, on the last Sunday of June 1977, printing workers held up production of *The Observer*. They disapproved of the wording of an advertisement about the Grunwick dispute which put the case of the management against the Association of Professional, Executive, Clerical and Computer Staff (APEX). This kind of censorship of the Press is spreading and will soon be imitated by journalists.

The National Union of Journalists, the principle journalists' union in Fleet Street, is heavily infiltrated by the Left Wing up to and including Communists, International

Socialists and the like. The official journal of the union has published without comment an article saying that the Press in Russia is freer than it is in Britain. Anyone with the slightest knowledge of politics knows what that implies. Resolutions are frequently passed within the union attempting to restrict members who report on such touchy subjects as racialism. By the nature of things it will not be very long before the N.U.J. seeks to establish by threat of strike the neutralization of editorial policies which its ultra Left Wing members dislike.

All around us the waves of tyranny are lapping away at the cliffs of freedom. A fall here and another there may seem to leave the majestic cliffs intact with but unimportant and unnoticed pieces gone. But the tiny falls cumulatively add up to a major erosion. They could also set off a vast and unstoppable avalanche.

The power of the leaders of the trade unions over a Labour Government is so great that they can demand outrageous manipulations of the law and nearly always attain them, though the Ministers concerned may be Social Democrats. But, as we have seen, the prime characteristics of the modern British Social Democrat is cowardice. When the T.U.C. demanded the release of the Shrewsbury pickets they confidently assumed that orders would be obeyed.

The Shrewsbury pickets were put in jail for organizing violent intimidation of building workers who would not instantly obey their instructions to stop work. Gangs of thugs were taken from site to site and peaceful workers were shaken off the scaffolding, and not a few were injured. Others were actually chased to their homes where they had to barricade themselves in to protect themselves from physical assault. In no possible way could the picketing have been described as peaceful or within the law.

Nevertheless, stimulated by the *Morning Star* and the Communist-dominated Liaison Committee for the Defence of Trade Unions, the T.U.C. decided to pose as a defender of democracy. With the aid of their allies on the Labour Party National Executive, now completely under the thumb of the very Left Wing trade-union leaders, an emergency

144

resolution was accepted at the Labour Party conference at the end of November 1974. It read,

This Conference rejects the reimprisonment of Bros. Tomlinson and Warren, the two remaining Shrewsbury pickets.

Conference believes that the sentences of two and three years which were imposed were a reflection of the anti-union hysteria which prevailed under the last Tory Government. These sentences were completely disproportionate to the offences for which the pickets were tried.

Therefore, Conference demands that the Home Secretary act immediately to release these men from prison.

The fury was that trade unionists had not yet been put completely above the law however much they might offend against even the criminal law. Winding up for the National Executive, Bryan Stanley said,

. . . that it is, in this case, the Home Secretary alone who has the power to recommend to the Queen the exercise of the Royal Prerogative, that is to set aside a conviction or remit part of a sentence. It is the intention of the N.E.C. to make representations to the Home Secretary . . .

The T.U.C. General Council has already been to see the Home Secretary and they have indicated this week that if a satisfactory answer is not obtained the General Council will continue the campaign and will take whatever steps are necessary in that continuation. In accepting this resolution therefore we will be expressing solidarity with the campaign being conducted by U.C.A.T.T. [the building workers' union] and with the T.U.C. representing ten million trade unionists.

The resolution designed to force the Home Secretary to release two convicted criminals because they claimed that their criminal actions were undertaken to further trade unionism was unanimously carried by the Labour Party conference. The T.U.C. and the ultra-Left Wing Labour Party National Executive expected no difficulty in persuading the Home Secretary to bend the law. After all Tony Crosland, as Minister for the Environment, had no scruples about bending it over the Clay Cross councillors, and he was a good Social Democrat.

The Clay Cross councillors had refused to carry out the provisions of a Rent Act on the grounds that it was passed by a Conservative Government and, since they were 'good' Socialists, they asserted that it had no validity in the area they controlled. Despite repeated warnings they were eventually taken to court where they were fined. This shocking notion that ultra-Left Wingers (which they were) should actually be penalized for breaking laws passed by a Tory Government filled the National Executive of the Labour Party with horror. They ordered the Government to alter the law retrospectively so that the offending Clay Cross councillors could add immunity to further charges in process against them to the martyrs' haloes they had already acquired. Naturally the Labour Party National Executive opened a fund to pay the fines already incurred. The Labour Government obligingly altered the law retrospectively to protect the councillors of Clay Cross from any further impertinent inquiry into their past illegal actions.

Yet when any person or group of persons is given freedom above the law the freedom of the rest of us is thereby lessened. It used to be said, somewhat inaccurately, that there was one law for the rich and one for the poor. It can now be said with greater accuracy that there is one law for trade unionists and ultra-Left Wingers and another for the rest of us.

However, to the amazement of the General Council of the T.U.C. and the Labour Party National Executive, the Home Secretary, Roy Jenkins, politely told them to go away when they confidently demanded his acquiescence in the release of the Shrewsbury pickets. No alteration was made to their prison sentences. Despite raucous clamour from the Communists and the very Left, from the T.U.C. and Labour's National Executive and all the Left Wing M.P.s, Roy Jenkins remained unmoved in the face of the numerous

T.U.C. delegations which called upon him. As a Social Democrat he believed in the rule of law and not bending it for political reasons.

Gradually the fuss died down but a small victory had been won for freedom. It was a remarkable illustration of the importance of courage in politics. If the other Social Democrats, who were in a majority in the Parliamentary Labour Party, had always been as resolute as Roy Jenkins it would have been possible to maintain Social Democracy as the main theme of Labour Party policy. If even the Social Democrats in the Cabinet of the 1974 Labour Government had been brave they could have thwarted and not enacted the Marxist measures brought before them. But the Social Democrats in the Labour Party have usually chosen to curry favour with the very Left in order not to be too unpopular to be given a ministerial post. In the act of such appeasement Social Democrats have regularly pretended, perhaps sometimes to themselves as well as at large, that things which should be anathema to a Social Democrat are acceptable.

Take the Dock Work Regulation Bill. Jack Jones, General Secretary of the Transport and General Workers' Union, has either had a special place in his heart for dockers, who form a section of his union, or has been mildly frightened by them, or both. On occasion they have barricaded him, mobbed him, hurled abuse and threatening gestures at him and have invaded his office in a highly alarming manner. The dockers are in the forefront in resisting industrial advances. New methods which speed up exports and imports and make them decisively cheaper are bitterly obstructed by the dockers.

For instance, they have successfully prevented the operation of container ships carrying self-propelled barges on the Humber and its adjacent inland waterways which were proved to be making imports cheaper and exports more competitive. But for their obstructive tactics, connived at by Jack Jones and the Government department sponsoring the statutory body controlling inland waterways, container ships carrying loaded barges, which could be discharged without unloading and reloading to sail on to

147

their ultimate destinations, would have been extended all over Britain. The Luddite dockers triumphed at the continuing cost of many millions a year to the British economy. The introduction of ships carrying loaded barges which need not be unloaded until the recipient actually received them would have lost them many superfluous jobs. It would also have lost them the ability, which they regard as a right, to pilfer from cargoes while they are being unloaded and reloaded. So another huge saving in preventing loss by theft would have been made by British industry.

Worried about the sending of goods abroad and their receipt here in prepacked containers which can be dealt with well inland from the ports, particularly at cold storage depots, the dockers ordered Jack Jones to instruct the Labour Government to give them control over this technical advance and priority in employment so that they could nullify its advantages. The dockers were not in the least bit concerned that the inland storage depots were far more efficient, productive and far less costly than using dockers at the ports. They were determined to preserve unnecessary and costly jobs requiring little skill and earning gross overpayment on the docks themselves. Hence the birth of the Dock Work Regulation Bill.

Under the quaint arrangements of this Bill any place within five miles of a waterway where packing and unpacking of cargoes took place was to be deemed a dock and to come under the provisions applying to employment of dockers. Consequently workers belonging to other unions were to give way to dockers, notoriously overpaid and inefficient, and to lose their own jobs. Or if they were lucky they might be admitted into the Dockers' Section of the Transport and General Workers' Union usually reserved for friends and relations of existing dockers.

This time freedom was to be denied not only to employers but to other trade unionists. Jack Jones, with the largest card vote at the T.U.C. and the Labour Party conference, was determined to force through this horrifying breach of democracy. What did the Social Democrats in the Parliamentary Labour Party do about it?

To begin with, absolutely nothing. No more than four in

the Cabinet opposed the Bill (though nineteen of them believed it wrong) which was then sent on its way through Parliament. Then flickers of protest began to stir. Trade unionists, other than dockers' representatives, started to complain though a trifle feebly as they were afraid of Jack Jones. Owners of cold storage depots got together and started a public campaign. Eventually, due principally to the opposition of two Labour M.P.s (John Mackintosh and Brian Walden) who dared to speak up and to abstain in a vital vote the five-mile limit was turned into a half-mile limit. The main provision of the Bill was thus effectively squashed in the Commons and remained squashed by the Lords.

In a narrowly divided House of Commons on an issue on which all the Opposition parties had combined it was possible for two Social Democrats in the Parliamentary Labour Party to force the Government to change their course but it was not done willingly. The bulk of the Social Democrat M.P.s remained pusillanimous and supported a Bill which they knew to be outrageous. Such an incident gives little hope of the Social Democrats in the Labour Party resisting the Marxist inroads encompassed by *Labour's Programme for Britain 1976* if there is a comfortable Labour majority in the House of Commons. Only the haphazard chance of a very narrow majority added to protests from trade-union sources was able to transform the character of the Dock Work Regulation Bill. Hardly a strong wall to defend us from inroads on our freedom.

The Social Democrats know that the 1974 Labour Government's proposals for employee participation in pension schemes are quite wrong. Originally it was planned that the trade unions should have the sole right of nominating the employee participants making up half the boards of pension schemes even in schemes which did not involve trade-union members at all. Later this arrogant proposal was diluted by a contemptuous concession. It was that trade unions would not have the sole right to appoint employee representatives in companies with no union members but would retain the sole right to appoint employee participants in companies even if they were only partly unionized.

149

Here there is no pretence of democracy. The employees intimately affected by what happens to pension schemes to which they belong are not to have any say as to who on the employees' side shall represent them. The trade unions will do that without any form of ballot and even in companies where only a handful of the employees belong to unions. The purpose is obvious. It is to enable the Left Wing extremists, Communists and their allies to get into a position where they can obstruct the proper commercial use of large pension funds. Knowing nothing of business, and being totally oblivious of the needs of the members of the pension scheme, and caring less, they will block any investment in firms which have interests in countries like South Africa, Chile, Brazil, Spain or in any other country which momentary Left Wing predilections cause them to dislike. They will probably also seek to put money into mad cooperative ventures and into anything with a Left Wing flavour about it and which is unlikely to make money.

They will not be responsible to an electorate so they cannot be thrown out however much damage they do to the interests of those they are allegedly representing. But they will have acquired more power of destruction and disruption in British industry. Taken by itself this may not appear to be a very large loss of freedom for millions of individuals in pension schemes. Nor has it received much publicity, presumably on the grounds that the public would not be much interested to read about it. Nevertheless to take away the present good management of pension funds upon which people depend for extra help in their retirement without consulting them and without regard to their wishes and to put that management into a crazy political arena is a very severe loss of freedom. The intended beneficiary is to be utterly helpless while inexperienced and ill-intentioned trade-union appointees damage his future livelihood.

So it goes on. Inch by inch. No inch perhaps very remarkable in itself but cumulatively marking a substantial step towards Marxist totalitarianism.

For instance, the clamour for fifty per cent employee participation on the boards of large companies is presented as industrial democracy. In fact it is the negation of and a complete misunderstanding of democracy plus a sure way of making the general standard of living lower than it otherwise might have been. The owners' right to deal with their property is taken away which, whatever else it may be, cannot conceivably be an extension of freedom but only an erosion of it. The commercial enterprise then becomes not a place where the management is given to those with the most commercial ability, drive, energy and foresight to make it profitable and grow for the benefit of shareholders and employees, but a place where the management has to be shared with those who are utterly opposed to management and to the idea of profits and efficiency. The commercial undertaking is to be treated not as something which survives, lives and expands by enterprise, drive and enthusiasm but as something which is to be reduced to the status of a nationalized industry and eventually to be nationalized as laid down in *Labour's Programme for Britain 1976.*

Other than altering the power structure in society, which Wedgwood Benn claims as a principal virtue for nationalization, there is no purpose in it. Between 1956 and 1972 the nationalized industries, despite their monopolistic position, lost £1,168 million. Between 1962 and 1972 the nationalized industries received over £6,500 million in subsidies with which they were still unable, overall, to make a profit. The net return on the assets used in nationalized industries has ranged between two and six per cent compared with eleven to nineteen per cent in privately owned and publicly quoted companies. The argument that nationalized industries' prices, and hence their profitability, have been artificially held down in the public interest is void. Prices in the nationalized industries have at all times risen, despite price restraint imposed by various Governments on them, *pari passu* with prices in the free-enterprise sector.

It is only when price restraint is removed that the nationalized industries make profits by price increases soaring above the rate of price increase in the free enterprise sector. These they are able to charge because there is no other supplier.

The 1977 ten per cent gas price increase was quite

151

unnecessary commercially since North Sea gas, in which the publicly owned gas undertakings have a monopoly, enabled them to make a profit without putting up their prices. The gas prices were put up to make the rising prices in the less efficiently run electricity industry look less awful. Not that it is the fault of those in the electricity industry that they are inefficient: they are frequently not allowed by the Government to use oil-fired stations which would be cheaper than subsidizing the nationalized coal industry to produce coal at an ever lower rate of productivity and far more expensively than it need be produced.

In 1975 nationalized electricity lost £265 million, the Post Office lost £304 million, and gas lost £44 million. In 1976 these losses were turned into profits by the simple expedient of putting up the prices beyond the level of the price increases in the privately owned sector, where of course as a result of the increases in the nationalized industries prices were pushed up higher than they otherwise would have gone.

However, the price rises which led to those profits did not help all the nationalized industries. British Steel in 1976 showed a loss of £264 million against a small profit of £89 million in the previous year; and a loss of £95 million for the financial year ending March 1977. We now import far more steel than we did before steel was nationalized. British Steel remains the least productive of the steel industries in the major industrial countries and is likely to continue to be so for many decades if, under the burden of nationalization, it ever makes any recovery at all.

The nationalized industries are in the happy position of having their huge loans and grants from the Government written off as though they had never been made. Even with this fantastic privilege they are unable to show consistent profits.

For example, British Rail lost £135 million in 1966, £153 million in 1967, £147 million in 1968, made a profit of £15 million and £10 million respectively in 1969 and 1970 (however did that happen?), returned to a loss of £15 million in 1971, a loss of £26 million in 1972, a loss of £52 million in 1973, a loss of £158 million in 1974, a loss of £61 million in 1975, and a loss of £30 million in 1976.

The idea that the nationalized industries can ever be as efficient as the private sector is a joke. While the nationalized industries paid only £81 million in taxes between 1962 and 1972 the private sector companies paid £13,729 million. Yet investment in the nationalized industries between 1948 and 1972 was about one-fifth of the entire total of national investment in fixed assets in the United Kingdom. They ought, therefore, to have been able to pay at least one-fifth as much to the Government in taxes as the private sector.

Government grants accounted for seven per cent of the amounts received on capital account by free enterprise companies for the period 1962–72. That compares with twenty-eight per cent for the nationalized industries. Pouring money into the nationalized industries and getting low productivity and inferior results has helped to hold back rises in the standard of living which would have taken place but for nationalization.

Nationalization has knocked between one and two per cent off our national growth rate. Taking a figure of three per cent a year growth rate over the last fifteen years (with one-fifth of our investment having gone into the nationalized industries) that growth could have been increased by between twenty-five and fifty per cent if we had not been encumbered by nationalization. We could have had an annual growth of four and a half to five per cent.

So when Social Democrats, weakly giving in to the Left Wing, claim that the nationalization of an industry like aircraft is irrelevant or unimportant they are talking through their hats. From contributing to the national growth rate and rising exports that industry will now be responsible for a lower growth rate and lower exports than otherwise would have occurred, thus reducing the standard of living below what it might have been. In 1977 the Labour Government took the aerospace industry out of the hands of two of our most brilliant businessmen – Sir Arnold Weinstock and Sir Arnold Hall. They put it under the control of sixty-five-year-old Lord Beswick who has never run a business in his life. This fantastic piece of bungling will lead inevitably to disaster yet the Social Democrats in the

Labour Cabinet and Parliamentary Labour Party pretended they thought this a good idea.

Let me put it another way. In the twenty years 1948 to 1968 the nationalized industries got an extra £7 of output (at 1958 prices) for every £100 worth of capital investment. The comparable figure for the free enterprise sector was £24 extra output for every £100 invested in capital or nearly three and a half times as much. That comparison allows for the fact that during this period of twenty years there was a reduction of thirty-three per cent in the numbers employed in the nationalized industries and an increase of sixteen per cent employed in the free enterprise manufacturing sector. By every measurement the nationalized industries have proved to be a failure when it comes to productivity and efficiency. They have even failed to protect jobs.

Nationalization has had a damping effect on our exports. We have been net importers of steel when we should have been net exporters. It could be argued that the virtually nationalized British Leyland (ninety-five per cent Government owned) is an export contributor. But it has done so badly that by mid 1977 over forty per cent of new cars sold in Britain were imported, thus creating new levels of negative exports in cars. British Leyland illustrates the evil effects of nationalization very well.

The *Report on the Future of the British Car Industry* by the Government's Central Policy Review Staff published in 1975 made a number of penetrating comments. It reported that:

The present competitive position of the British car industry is poor. This relative inefficiency has emerged in the past fifteen years and the slide is continuing. In 1955 the United Kingdom industry accounted for over a quarter of world production outside the United States. Today it accounts for only ten per cent.

Incidentally, in 1965 the British car industry had ninety-five per cent of the United Kingdom market and now has less than sixty per cent.

The same Report recorded,

British productivity per man is far below the levels in the E.E.C. British wage rates are lower but not enough to compensate. British productivity has not changed in the past decade, while our competitors have improved their productivity and will continue to do so. We are particularly bad in assembly, where the labour requirements for assembling the same car, even with *identical capital equipment,* are nearly double. In engines it is fifty to sixty per cent more.

The Report notes some of the main causes of this low labour productivity, for instance,

Overmanning – In some operations fifty to eighty per cent more than on the Continent, even when both job and equipment are identical.

Slower work pace – Slower line speeds, late starts, frequent stoppages, bad work practices.

Poor maintenance – British plants need fifty to seventy per cent more maintenance men, yet lose twice as many production hours due to breakdowns, even when capital equipment is identical in age with that on the Continent.

At British Leyland the management have to deal with seventeen unions and in 1977 were dealing with 126 bargaining groups set up by those unions. Not a day passes without some form of negotiation between management and union representatives taking place for agreements which end and start at different times. All this discussion makes smooth management impossible. It contrasts sharply with Germany, for example, where there is only one union and one yearly agreement throughout the whole motor industry. In most of our competitor countries there are not more than two unions in the motor industry, thus making management a more constructive activity. The situation in British Leyland, which was bad before the Government became the ninety-five per cent owner, has since got worse. The dramatic devaluation of the pound plus the relatively lower wages paid in Britain have been unable to prevent an increase of imported foreign motor cars coming in over the

155

top of the pound's devaluation which by itself should have been sufficient to price them out of the British home market.

Strikes have been wantonly entered upon in the correct belief that the Government dare not allow so large a firm to go under whatever may be said officially to the contrary. British Leyland employees enjoy the splendid advantage shared by other employees in the nationalized industries: the Government stands behind the boards which run them with a bottomless well of taxpayers' money. They cannot lose their jobs by striking through the company running out of funds. The strikers are in the jolly position of knowing that the nationalized industry they work for, and the Government, will give in at the end, continuing to subsidize them however uneconomic they are. Thus the miserable taxpayer has lost the freedom to sack those who work for him, and do not report for work. Thus the exports which could have been won by British Leyland are much lower than they might have been, as will be the exports of the aircraft industry and shipbuilding in due course.

In exports nationalization is a bad performer as in every other field. The more it is extended the fewer will be our exports. In 1973 our exports represented 23.4 per cent of our domestic output — a higher figure than Canada, West Germany, France, Japan or the U.S.A. Ninety-five per cent of the exports of British goods came from the free enterprise sector and nearly as high a proportion of our export of services.

The volume of the United Kingdom export of goods was seventy-seven per cent higher in 1973 then it was in 1963 – a high level from which we are rapidly falling through the extension of nationalization. The much derided and complained of investments by British companies overseas brought in an income in 1973 of one-quarter the total of our exports of goods and services.

The ultra-Left Wing as soon as they can get their hands on that aspect of our economy will sell off British investments overseas for a short-lived propping up of public spending at home and will prevent any such further investment. The excuse will be that any money companies have available for investment should be invested at home to provide jobs for

British workers, ignoring the fact that frequently a better return can be got from investment overseas than in Britain and that many foreign governments demand a substantial investment in their country by any foreign firm wishing to export to them.

I repeat: the reason for more nationalization is to give very Left Wing politicians more power and to diminish our freedom of choice whether in the variety of employment available to us or in the goods offered for sale.

The Marxists do not think it matters that the absence of profit motive, or of a balance sheet in which shareholders are concerned, encourages waste, overmanning, careless costing and pricing, lack of interest in modernization and contributes to an inevitable decline in almost every industry which is nationalized. In Russia and the Eastern European countries the performance of industry does not even come up to British Leyland standards where memories of, and habits from, what was done under free enterprise still linger on. If the facts were known and disseminated within and without the Communist countries about the inferior performance of State-owned industry compared with free enterprise industry there would be no problem about persuading people that the Marxists are not merely malevolent but mad. It would not be necessary to have a wall in Berlin and troops and guard posts with barbed wire lining the frontier of East Germany to prevent East Germans escaping to the West if the economic situation in East Germany were comparable with that in West Germany. Even so, in East Germany families divided by the artificial boundary between East and West Germany do, however, contrive to communicate across it. So East Germans are better informed than most of the other subjects of the Russian empire.

The ultra-Left Wing are not troubled by the prospect that the power given to the State by additional nationalization may from time to time be exercised by Conservatives or a combination of parties which does not include Labour. They are confident that if they cannot force through the T.U.C. proposals (cravenly endorsed by Bullock) that half the boards of the large free-enterprise companies should consist of trade-union appointees they will nevertheless be able to force them through in the public sector.

In 1977 the Post Office Corporation itself proposed a major sell-out in this direction, thus making it clear that they regard the chief function of the board running the Post Office Corporation as not to make money and to provide a better public service but to placate the trade-union leaders whose attitude, due to the way their minds have been conditioned in this country, must always be inimical to good management. This pattern will be servilely followed in other nationalized industries so that the trade-union appointees, mainly from the ultra-Left, will be able to exercise considerable economic influence, even when the Labour Party which they nominally support is out of office. The more that workers' participation leading to workers' control, and operated by the ultra-Left, can be extended, the less it will matter who wins the elections at Westminster.

Taken in conjunction with the infiltration of non-elected unrepresentative trade-union appointees on local councils, in the governing bodies of educational establishments including universities, in the Civil Service and the National Health Service, the aim is a formidable burrowing into the democratic structure of society. The outside will continue to have a reassuring appearance of familiarity. The inside is due to be devoured and seized by the termites while elected representatives become secondary figures meaninglessly performing ritual dances on the surface.

CHAPTER TWELVE

What is to be Done?

THE DETERIORATION has gone very far. Attitudes of mind have been fixed in mis-shapen moulds. As I have illustrated throughout this book assumptions are made which are perversions of the truth. Workers' control, which is another name for tyranny by unelected or defectively elected ultra-Left Wingers, is called industrial democracy.

To incite envy and to justify further swipes at the wealth creators *Labour's Programme for Britain 1976* says 'The richest one per cent of the population owns nearly thirty per cent of the nation's privately owned wealth.' The Royal Commission on the Distribution of Income and Wealth in Report No. 4 presented in October 1976 says something quite different.

After assessing the value of State pension rights the top one per cent in 1974 owned only 13.8 per cent of privately owned wealth. The figure would be still lower if estates not exceeding £15,000 exempted from capital transfer tax on death were included in the global figures instead of the curious assumption being made that anyone who pays no capital transfer tax on death has no possessions at all, which is ludicrous. By 1977 inflation and increased taxation had seen to it that the top one per cent and the top twenty per cent had a much smaller share of privately owned wealth than they had in 1974. But the exaggeration about the wealth held by a few must be repeated to perpetuate the myth.

Censorship of the Press is called workers' participation. The denial of the right to spend your money as you wish, for example on private medicine, is called an extension of democracy. Restrictive practices in industry are called the legitimate rights of employees to protect themselves against unemployment. Terrorism on building sites leading to prison sentences, or mob violence outside the Grunwick factory in the summer of 1977, is called peaceful picketing. The capturing of important official posts in the Labour Party and the trade unions by tiny, unrepresentative and malevolent minorities is called expressing the people's will. The prevention of secret postal ballots in union affairs is called protecting union members from undemocratic outside interference. Minority Governments elected with less than forty per cent of the popular vote are held to have been given a mandate by the people to implement manifestos which they have not read. The nationalization of industries is claimed to be for the benefit of those who work in them but every survey taken in an industry about to be nationalized shows an overwhelming majority of its employees opposed to the nationalization. And labour relations in the nationalized industries are no better, if not actually worse, than in the private sector.

Block votes wielded at Labour Party conferences by a handful of trade-union leaders who have not consulted their members, or ascertained their wishes, are described as the epitome of representative democracy. The selection of ultra-Left Wing Labour candidates by tiny local caucuses who have views alien to ninety per cent of Labour voters is called acting in the people's name. The confiscation of unnecessarily large amounts of the individual's earnings to be wasted on extravagant and often useless public expenditure is described as the social wage. And so on.

Anyone who describes situations as they actually are rather than in fantasy terms is reactionary or Right Wing or possibly Fascist. Managements and employers remain the wicked and heartless landlords of Victorian melodrama, ruthlessly exploiting the workers. Whereas today it is the employers and managements who are exploited by many of the workers, though the workers may have been misled into the role by ultra-Left Wing trade-union leaders.

To stop the dangerous slide towards becoming the replica of an East European state we must wake up to what is going on. We must stop seeing the various Marxist manoeuvres as isolated instances with no special significance in themselves

160

and start to see them as a whole related to a plan to push us beyond the point of no return without our noticing it. We must understand that the Labour Party was solidly Social Democratic between 1945 and 1951, wobbled a bit until Gaitskell became Leader in 1955, and was then restored to a firm Social Democratic condition until Gaitskell's death in 1963, remaining reasonably Social Democratic until 1970, and succumbing badly to the Marxists' assaults after 1970.

Outwardly, with Callaghan and a majority of ostensible Social Democrats in a Labour Cabinet, or apparently leading the Party, the rind may look much the same. Under the rind the fruit has been nearly destroyed by the maggots. As I hope by this time I have made plain there is always a time-lag between the change of effective control in a Party and the moment the public realizes that this has happened. The longer the public remains in darkness the more dangerous it is and the more difficult it becomes to halt the slide.

The 1977 pact between the Labour Government and the Liberal M.P.s halted the Labour Government's implementation of the wishes of the extremists. The moderate and reasonable behaviour thus forced upon the Labour Government probably made many forget how alarming their behaviour was before the pact with the Liberals. Like rabbits just escaped from under the wheels of a motor car our previous fright vanishes and we believe the world to be a safe place again. But we must not forget that both the Social Democrats and the extremists in the Labour Party detest restraint from the Liberals. They long to have a clear Labour majority in Parliament so that the same course can be followed as before.

As I said at the beginning, it was correct for a Social Democrat to vote Labour in 1945. It was still correct in 1964. It was defensible to do so in 1970 when, if Labour had won, the impetus which is given to the Marxists in Opposition would not have been there. It cannot be desirable to vote Labour now, if you value democracy, let alone Social Democracy. It will not be desirable to vote Labour for at least the next ten years.

Many who are worried about our drift towards an East European style dictatorship controlled by Communists,

161

Marxists and the ultra-Left feel helpless. They ask, what then must be done to halt the slide and to re-establish democracy? They want to know how the tiny minorities of extremists can be excluded from positions which enable them to take actions opposed by the great majority.

The obvious answer is that everyone who is a Social Democrat, or merely a democrat, should take a full part in the activities of his trade union and local political party. After all, approximately one-third of trade unionists vote Conservative. If they alone set out to capture the trade-union machinery in the same determined way as the five to ten per cent extremists who are trade-union members have done then they too could do it. The obstructive attitudes of the trade unions in industry and the unhealthy domination of the Labour Party by ultra-Left Wing union leaders would cease. There would be the same result if the ordinary Labour voters, who are also trade unionists, attended their branch meetings and saw to it that official positions went to those of their persuasion and not to extremists eager to have them. But this is an impossibility. The ordinary person shrinks from participation in long meetings where the boredom is only lifted when abusive attacks are made upon him by strident but able extremists. He prefers to watch television or go out in his motor car.

If ordinary Labour voters joined their local Labour Parties in large numbers and elected each other to man the Labour Party constituency committees and offices they would control the selection of the candidates and be able to rid themselves of Marxist and extremist Labour M.P.s masquerading as Social Democrats. But they will not do so because they prefer to spend their leisure in more agreeable ways. To ask the generality of people to preserve their democratic heritage by doing something prolonged and dedicated about it is as hopeless as it is for an archbishop to exhort people to go to church. When their democratic heritage has been dissipated beyond recall they will regret that they did nothing to save it. By then it will be too late.

Here and there groups of democrats do fight back winning successes disproportionate to their numbers. But

162

such sporadic efforts can no more be relied upon to preserve our democracy than the Social Democrats in the Parliamentary Labour Party can be relied upon to put their seats and jobs at risk by conducting a resolute fight against the extremists in their midst. In a congenial democracy such as ours, where life is still very pleasant, it is useless to expect a consistent effort from democrats to uphold their faith if doing so puts them to inconvenience.

So to the question: What then must be done by individuals?, I can give only one answer. It is that they must vote Conservative however distasteful and unfamiliar the prospect may be to many. We can no longer gloss over the two clear alternatives which face the country in the immediate future. Either we shall be governed by Marxists, acting through the Labour Party, or we shall be governed by Conservatives.

Voting Liberal, under our present first-past-the-post electoral system, cannot resolve this dilemma. It is an act of escapism in the hope that somehow or other a sufficient number of Liberals will get into the House of Commons to restrain the Labour Party from extremism. But so long as we have no proportional representation this is quite impossible. All that voting Liberal will do is to make it more likely than otherwise that there will be a Labour Government dominated by Marxists. To vote Liberal, alas, is to be as feeble as those Social Democrats in the Parliamentary Labour Party who know what they should be saying and doing but dare not. If the threat to democracy were not so great it would be defensible for democrats to vote Liberal but in the present difficult climate it is nothing more than dodging the issue and refraining from making a decision between Marxism and democracy because of a dainty distaste for the Conservatives.

The Conservatives have many defects but they have had one virtue for a very long time. Those firmly in charge of the Conservative Party genuinely believe in the democratic process as it has been understood for generations in Britain. The protection of our democracy must now take precedence over all other questions and the only way to ensure it is not to dally with hopes that there will be enough Liberals, or

Social Democrats, in the Parliamentary Labour Party, to save it. The naturally lazy democrat can at least go to a polling booth and vote for democracy, effectively represented at the moment only by the Conservatives, and refrain from voting for the Labour Party, now incapable of defending democracy from its own extremists, or for the Liberals who cannot conceivably get enough seats to do anything about it. The logic is inescapable.

The Labour Party must have the shock of going into the wilderness for a long time – at least for two Parliaments. The Social Democrats in it would then apprehend that the tactic of appeasing the Marxists and the extreme Left Wing in order to present an apparently united Party to win elections has exhausted itself. The preposterous coalition between the Social Democrats (whose approach is little different from one-third of the Conservative M.P.s and all of the Liberal M.P.s) and the Marxists, Trotskyists and other extremists might then collapse. Social Democrats believe in changes being made only when there is a genuine majority for them and in this respect they are no different from Conservatives or Liberals. Social Democrats do not believe that the power of the State is more important than the liberty of the individual. The Marxists, Trotskyists and other extremists in the Labour Party, on the contrary, believe that the people are not competent to choose what is best for them but must have a Socialist system imposed upon them. Hence they are little different from outright members of the Communist Party.

On 28 June 1977 Syd Bidwell, a prominent member of the Tribune Group of Labour M.P.s, wrote in the *Morning Star,* 'I find my differences with the Communist Party nowadays . . . negligible.' Mainly he differs with the Communist Party's programme *The British Road to Socialism* where it states, 'We believe we can achieve Socialism in Britain without civil war.' Syd Bidwell writes, 'While I mainly accept this, I wish to be less categorical. I too believe the class forces in Britain should be strong enough to avoid civil war in the transition to Socialism. I do not rule it out. It could well be avoided on the way up to people's power, but counter-revolutionary activities successful in other countries . . . cannot be removed from the mind or from advanced thinking and planning.' In other words Syd Bidwell speaks the full jargon of the Communist dictator and it is not acceptable that Social Democrats should remain with him and those of his views in the same Labour Party. It must be the aim of the ordinary voter to make it impossible. If Hugh Gaitskell were alive I am sure that he would have led a successful breakaway of the Social Democrats from the Labour Party long ago.

The Social Democrats have nothing in common with the rest of the Labour Party except a joint membership of an organization called the Labour Party and the hope that in combination they may deceive the public into believing that the Labour Party is still Social Democratic and thus win office. The real home for the Marxists and their allies is in a separate Communist Party in which they could openly declare their true beliefs instead of dissembling about them as they do today. The electorate would then no longer vote for men and women indistinguishable from Communists in their views, on the naive supposition that they are genuine Social Democrats of the Attlee or Gaitskell or Callaghan variety.

The break-up of the present Labour Party is the most important step towards ensuring the continuation of our democratic society and the maintenance of free enterprise under conditions which will allow it to flourish for the benefit of the nation. Unless the Labour Party is broken up the mixed economy will become an economy dominated by unproductive nationalization and our society will inevitably be run on Eastern European lines.

A prerequisite is a landslide, or massive, victory for the Conservatives at the next election. A narrow anti-Labour majority would not destroy the extreme Left Wingers. It would stimulate them to argue more fiercely that the reason Labour lost was because the manifesto was not Socialist enough. The false Labour coalition would be preserved. It is a false coalition because there is no real identity of outlook between the extremists and the rest whatever synthetic attempts may be made to prove otherwise.

The anti-Labour majority must be large enough and, if

possible, of 1931 proportions to embolden the Social Democrats in the Labour Party to start breaking away from those who would be happier in Eastern Europe or at the very least in an Italian or French style Communist Party. To help the Social Democrats keep their courage up, not just the next election but the succeeding election should produce a massive anti-Labour majority. And Labour's defeats must continue until the Labour Party has purged itself of the Marxists, Trotskyists and undercover Communists and their allies.

There is no doubt that the Social Democratic elements in the Parliamentary Labour Party and among the leadership represent more than ninety per cent of the Labour voters. If this is questioned consider that no opinion poll on nationalization shows more than ten per cent of Labour voters in favour of more large-scale nationalization. That is the position of the Social Democrats and not that of the Marxist extremists and the ultra-Left Wing in the Labour Party. That is a good foundation on which to build. But how would a newly constituted Social Democrat Party with most of the respected Labour leaders in it finance itself? The trade unions provide the great bulk of the Labour Party's funds. The leaders of some of the richest unions would tend to follow the Marxists and the extremists rather than the Social Democrats.

There is a simple solution which is employed in West Germany and other democratic countries. It is to provide the funds needed to keep political parties functioning and campaigning out of public monies. Each party should be allotted public money in proportion to the number of votes it received at the previous election provided that the main Opposition party always receives the same amount as the main Government party. A minimum level of total votes should be set below which no public money would be allotted to discourage fringe and lunatic parties. It could happen that a party like the National Front or the Communist Party, infected by a disagreeable virus of racialism or totalitarianism, became entitled to an official subvention. This would have to be accepted.

It should be illegal for any person or organization to

subscribe to a political party. The subventions should be set sufficiently high to make this unnecessary. The effect would be entirely beneficial. No great party would be in the position of having to satisfy its paymasters. Government could become more impartial in the interests of the nation as a whole rather than in the interests of sections.

Business and free enterprise would remain the natural ally of the Conservative Party but even the mildest blackmail from the present donors would vanish.

The help to Social Democrats either in the present Labour Party or in a new party which might arise would be enormous. The problem of where the funds are to come from if the Social Democrats go it alone or form an alliance with the Liberals and part of the Conservative Party would be gone. This would apply even if the assets of the official Labour Party had not been captured by the Social Democrats but had been captured by the ultra-Left. Public subvention of political parties might even make it unnecessary for the Social Democrats to break away from the Labour Party. The union leaders could throw their block votes about at Labour Party conferences however they liked and could be totally ignored by the Parliamentary Labour Party and the Labour leadership because the union leaders would have lost the use of the threat to withhold their cash if their orders are not obeyed.

At the same time as subventions for the political parties were introduced the unions would lose their legal right to collect a levy from their members to be paid into a political purposes fund. Trade unionists would be saved the embarrassment of having specifically to opt out of paying that political levy if they do not like the uses to which it is put.

Subventions to the political parties would be a trivial cost to pay towards preserving our democracy and preventing the political parties (particularly the Labour Party) being held in thrall by extremist minorities. At 1977 prices not more than £5 million a year would be needed. It would be necessary to top this up by some £1½ million in an election year to enable all the political parties to put out their maximum effort in propaganda.

The suggestion that political parties would receive all their funds from the State and none from other sources is less impracticable than it was a few years ago. Recently Lord Houghton's official committee has made respectable the idea that the political parties should receive State money to help them in some of their functions. Once that principle is conceded there becomes nothing disreputable about the State giving money to the political parties for all their reasonable activities.

However, even if the political parties depended on no outside organizations, including the trade unions, for their cash the trade-union leaders would still exert an unrepresentative influence in Labour Party counsels and upon the Government of the day and on matters central to the economy. It is therefore essential that all the unions become organized on democratic lines. A landslide Conservative victory would give the Conservative Government moral power to act in this direction, particularly if they got a second term with another large majority.

There must be compulsory secret ballots paid for by the State and conducted from start to finish by impartial outside bodies when important officers are chosen and important decisions are made. There must also be some means of removing or confirming in office those important officials who are elected for life. For instance, Moss Evans, elected General Secretary of the Transport and General Workers' Union in 1977, cannot be dislodged until 1991 when he is due to retire at the age of 65. He may be very good but such absolute power, so significant to the future of the country, can turn the head of many a man who starts out with a modest attitude. It is hard for him to remain democratic if, whatever he does, he cannot be challenged. It is also obvious, as I have already described, that the relationship of the General Secretary to the governing body of the Transport and General Workers' Union is such that before long the General Secretary, provided he has a bare minimum of purpose and personality, is bound to dominate. The block vote of the nearly two million strong Transport and General Workers' Union is, until 1991, due to be wielded at Moss Evans's dictate. This could be a great improvement on its being wielded by Jack Jones – on the other hand it may not be.

In the interests of individual freedom compulsory extensions to the closed shop must be forbidden though it is too late to do anything about those closed shops which already exist, except in the Press where it is vital that the closed-shop principle should be abandoned. It should in any case be illegal to compel a man to join a union merely because a closed shop has arrived at his work place.

Consideration, too, should be given to operating a similar rule to that in America which prevents sympathetic strikes by people in other places of work not connected with the dispute whether they are in the same union or not. Removal of the power to black nationally the products and supplies of a firm with which a local workforce is officially or unofficially in dispute would give some strength to managements seeking to resist unreasonable wage claims or trying to introduce systems for increased productivity.

All strikes, whether official or unofficial, should also be illegal unless they have been preceded by a secret strike ballot in which the strike is approved by at least fifty-five per cent of those voting (as is the practice in strike ballots conducted by the National Union of Mineworkers). In the same vein strikes during the period of an agreement should be made illegal and disputes arising before the expiry of an agreement should be settled by industrial courts.

None of the foregoing is reactionary or oppressive. These measures are standard procedures in West Germany where the Social Democrats have ruled successfully for years. They would, of course, limit the power for mischief of the trade-union leaders whether inside the Labour Party or outside. But the power of the irresponsible trade-union leaders (irresponsible because they are not responsible to properly constituted electorates) should be curbed just as the State in previous times had had to curb the power of the King, of the Church leaders, the barons, the landlords and the industrialists.

It is quite ridiculous that the trade-union leaders not only pontificate on issues which do not concern them such as what to do about Chile but that their opinions on all manner of subjects of which they have no knowledge or understanding are taken seriously. The trade unions must be pushed by public opinion out of politics and back to their real role of bettering pay and conditions for their members. In politics a trade unionist has no more right to exercise a role than a chartered accountant or a junior manager. He may be listened to as a normal lobbyist is listened to on matters affecting his profession or occupation but not on political matters that have nothing to do with the way in which he earns his living.

Originally it was necessary for the trade unions to help in the creation of the Labour Party so that their views could be expressed and attended to on trade-union affairs in the House of Commons. There was no recognition of their great importance or rights. But now recognition that they have a definite status in relation to their members' conditions and pay has turned to subservience in far too many areas. Jack Jones is accepted as an authority on what happens in Spain or Brazil. No businessman is.

What I have suggested so far, even if it were implemented, is not sufficient to prevent minority Governments, controlled by minorities within their own party, putting through extremist legislation resented by over three-quarters of the population and deleterious to the nation. One innovation which would aid Social Democrats and common-sense M.P.s taking an objective and not over-partisan line would be the institution of primaries. This would enable members threatened by extremists dominating their local caucus to secure reselection as a candidate and would enable moderately minded candidates to challenge the tenure of extremist M.P.s.

Primaries are not expensive to organize: certainly they are far cheaper than local government elections. They work very effectively in America. They need only be called for when there is some doubt among the supporters of a party as to the desirability of an official party candidate. He can then be challenged by a candidate of the same party, with a different approach, for a decision as to who goes forward as the official party candidate in the election proper.

Primaries would require Parliaments to serve for a fixed

170

term of, say, four or five years. This would be necessary so that there could be a timed programme during which demands could be made and met for a primary in a constituency, and a date fixed. Voting in primaries to choose the standard-bearer for a particular party should be confined to those registered as supporters of the party concerned. There would not be a large number in each constituency but there would be far more than the tiny group which form the selection committee caucuses in constituency parties at present.

There is a growing appreciation that the way in which the House of Commons is elected does not reflect the views of the electors. In the October election of 1974 some form of proportional representation would have given the Liberals 100 seats or more instead of the thirteen seats they won. Millions of voters are accordingly disenfranchised by our present system. Worse than that they, and moderate opinion in both the major parties, see that, by the first-past-the-post system under which the winner takes all, it is increasingly possible for minorities within the winning group (principally the Labour Party) to force through legislation and measures which have the support often of no more than ten per cent of the population. This is not democracy. It is dangerous lunacy.

The two great parties would not like to change to some form of proportional representation. Their hope would then be gone of forming Governments based on majorities in the House of Commons despite their having a minority of votes in the country. When the Labour Government was defeated in 1970 the Labour Party won 43 per cent of the votes cast. Yet it was able to form Governments in the 1974 elections of February and October with 37.2 per cent of the votes and 39.3 per cent of the votes respectively. What was far short of sufficient in 1970 had become enough in 1974.

Naturally it would be inconvenient for the two main parties to be obliged on many occasions to form a coalition with the Liberals, or other third party, if they wished to have a majority in Parliament. But it happens very satisfactorily in West Germany and other Continental countries. Proportional representation is a powerful safeguard against

171

extremist or highly partisan measures being put through by minority governments against majority opinion. The demand to be more correctly represented in Parliament will grow. It will have to be conceded some time so why not now before more damage is done to the structure of Britain?

Another important advantage of some form of proportional representation would be the effect upon the Labour Party. It would be much easier for sincere Social Democrats to be elected and it would be much easier for them to form an association with the Liberal Party, who in the main are Social Democrats who have never subscribed to rigid lines of direction and who are mainly animated by a vague dislike of Conservatives to which they frequently allow precedence over their dislike of the Labour Party because they have not perceived the nature of the ir-removable grip which the Marxists, the ultra-Left, the extremists and their Communist allies have upon it.

A very respectable party could be formed, with the aid of proportional representation, by a merging of the Liberals and Social Democrats. We must have some thoroughly democratic alternative to the Conservative Party which we do not have today. This is the only way in which it could arise.

Again, even the safeguard of some form of proportional representation by a single transferable vote system or whatever device is chosen, may not be strong enough to prevent unpopular and undesirable measures being forced through by minorities of minority governments. To make assurance double sure the practice of holding referendums should be introduced. It was applied with great success over Britain's continued membership of the European Economic Community in 1975. The Left Wing extremists never cease to speak of the right of ordinary people to express their view. Although they mean by this that they are the custodians of the views of the people who cannot be expected to have any views dissimilar to their own (or to express them other than through the ultra-Left Wing) they would nevertheless be in difficulties in opposing referen-dums on important subjects.

When Parliament consisted of representatives responsive more to their own judgment and to public opinion than to the orders of their party whips referendums were not needed so much as they are today. But again and again Parliament passes or accepts measures which on a free vote of the House of Commons would not have been carried. Though sometimes, as on the issue of proportional representation when there may be a free vote, that free vote deliberately flouts the popular opinion because of the self-interest of politicians afraid of disturbing the convenient current arrangements.

In Switzerland a referendum can be demanded on any subject. They are frequently held successfully. It is not enough to say that Switzerland is a smaller country than Britain. The difficulty of holding a referendum by regions is no greater in Britain than it is in Switzerland.

It should be possible, after the collection of, say, 100,000 signatures to petition Parliament (which would have to agree) for a referendum. The right to demand a referendum should concern the principle of major legislation or the use of Government powers involving any major new nationalization and to broad questions affecting the liberty of the subject. The latter could include such items as abortion law, divorce law, Sunday entertainments, public house opening hours, automatic licensing of cafes to serve drinks, employee directors, the closed shop, the compulsory wearing of seat belts, the prevention of cigarette smoking and so forth.

Effective democracy would incidentally be widened and people would feel that they had some say in their own affairs other than recording a vote at uncertain intervals in general elections. Modern electronics could make carrying out a referendum a simple matter for the organizers and simple for the voters.

It could not be truthfully argued that referendums would place an unreasonable burden on the people. In some unions members are required at frequent intervals to vote on twenty or thirty positions for various offices in their unions. Shareholders of companies are also invited to cast their votes very often. If a voter does not want to use his vote on an important subject, that is up to him but at least he would have been given the opportunity. The putting of a wide variety of subjects to the general public would in practice increase interest in politics and make discussions on issues of the day more meaningful.

Another safeguard against extremism would be a reformed House of Lords. In its present unrepresentative state it is without the authority even to use its brief delaying powers except on very special occasions. A House of Lords with members elected for a fixed term of, say, six years with one third coming up for election every two years would be a body which would have the moral right not merely to use the short delaying powers it has now but to be given additional powers. The members of such a newly constituted House of Lords should be elected regionally on some form of proportional representation and there need not be more than 200 of them. The elected members alone should be allowed to vote in the Lords though there would be no objection to hereditary and life peers taking part in debates without the right to vote.

A Second Chamber which refreshed itself every two years in such a manner would give the electorate a valuable chance to express its opinion in between general elections. It should be allowed to hold up Bills for at least three years and in doing so would democratically reflect the current opinion of the voters. A Conservative Government with a large majority should give immediate consideration to democratic reform of the Lords so that the Second Chamber can exercise a restraint on extremists whether from the Right or the Left.

If it is thought that what I have suggested till now would tend towards consensus in government, so much the better. It is the illusion of partisan party politicians that there is some great merit in a perpetual clash between violent opposites. This is not the case. The swinging about that occurs on changes of government is unsettling and not wished for by the people. They would prefer courses to be followed on which there is maximum agreement not maximum disagreement. They would also like to see those of the Labour, Conservative and Liberal Parties of a similar frame of mind leave their artificial cages and join together.

The electors would be quite content to see the others, more extreme, forming one or more opposition parties.

The people are not normally vindictive or envious except in sections and when they are stirred up by the mischievous to be so. Most people think, for instance, that we have now gone too far in penalizing the wealth creators. They think we have gone too far in nationalization. The first task of a Conservative Government must be to reverse these trends so far as is practicable. The Conservatives should immediately reduce taxation on earned income and on capital transfers before and after death to the levels prevailing in the U.S.A. and the European Economic Community. It is still possible to denationalize some large units and to denationalize parts of aerospace. If some form of proportional representation is introduced, denationalization can be made to stick. If it is not, a future Labour Government would still have to spend most of its Parliamentary time renationalizing the denationalized and thus be debarred from fresh exploits in this arena.

Most people believe that employees should have more say about what happens in the places where they work but they would like to do it in a British way. That is, by an evolutionary process beginning with properly constituted and efficient works councils and a few employee directors on boards to see whether increased employee participation would increase the strength of a large company and not lessen it. They do not want new departures in this field clumsily rammed through by the blunt orders of the T.U.C.

Despite occasional excesses we are civilized and tolerant. We are not suited to government by loud-mouthed minorities restlessly destroying what has been proved worthwhile with the unlikely aim of replacing it with something better after their work of destruction is completed.

Though we have been involved in two world wars in this century, and have now joined the European Economic Community, we are vaguely confident that nothing cataclysmic can happen to us. Just as for years we did not consciously register the full impact of the Hitler menace so today we find it hard to believe that Left Wing extremists

175

have captured the Labour Party after they have actually done so.

We take our freedom of speech and of individual action so much for granted that we do not detect the very potent threats to them. Each curtailment of liberty and choice that occurs we regard as an isolated, not to be repeated instance. That is why we have slid so far towards an Eastern European style state without the strong protests we would have made if we had understood where we were being taken.

Fortunately, as I have indicated, we have the remedy at our disposal. The longer we delay in applying it the worse the disease will be and the more difficult it will be to eradicate it. I started this book by explaining why it was right to vote Labour in the past and wrong now. I said that no one need feel shame at lost ideals by switching his vote from the Labour Party in the next election. It is the Labour Party (I hope temporarily) which has lost its ideals and needs a long period without office in which to learn to recover them. It must become again the party of Attlee and Gaitskell.

If the Conservative Party wins by the handsome majority they need to take us away from the edge below which lies Eastern Europe, the Conservative Party must in turn learn not to trample over the feelings of the millions who have voted Labour. They must learn that compromise is not weakness. They must learn that though perfect social justice is unattainable the attempt to attain it should not be abandoned. When, for instance, they reduce the highest rate of income tax, as I hope they will, to a fifty per cent limit they must do it in such a way as to benefit most those who work hard and productively and create national wealth. The purpose should not be to encourage property speculation and the shuffling of pieces of paper which brings large gains not from serious work but from the successful use of a gambler's instinct.

It is possible to reduce the number of employees in the National Health Service and save public money while at the same time improving the efficiency of the service to the public. By not filling every vacancy that occurs, the Civil Service and the local government service can eventually be brought to acceptable levels of manning without the harshness of enforced redundancies.

It is of prime importance that the next Conservative Government should be conducted humanely and efficiently and with regard to the interests of the people as a whole whether they be in trade unions or have nothing to do with them. The ideal should be to create an administration similar to, but not a copy of, that of the Social Democratic Government in Germany.

The Conservatives will have difficulty in dealing with some trade-union leaders. They will only overcome that difficulty by proving to trade-union members that a Conservative Government is as concerned about their welfare as a Labour Government and more skilful in achieving it.

It is not too late to arrest our relative industrial decline and restore liberties which have been lost. It can be done if there is a Government brave enough to initiate and follow through the right actions. At the present juncture only a Conservative Government has the potential to do this. The responsibility placed upon it would be enormous. If the Conservatives win and then do so badly that they are defeated at the end of their first term of office our democracy will be unlikely to survive. The successor Labour Government would be openly ultra-Left Wing and almost certainly led by an extremist. They would feel no restraints upon themselves in pursuing the Marxist aims of the dominant voices in the Labour Party.

Nor would Britain alone be in danger. The Communist Parties of Italy and France are edging nearer to effective power in or upon their Governments. If Britain has an ultra-Left Wing Government the will of Western Europe to withstand Soviet encroachment will evaporate to the point where America may feel it not worth helping us to defend ourselves. Not for the first time, the lead which Britain gives to Europe in defending democracy could be decisive.

INDEX

179

181